BELGRADE AND BEYOND: THE CSCE PROCESS IN PERSPECTIVE

East-West Perspectives, 5

General editor
James A. Kuhlman, University of South Carolina, USA

BELGRADE AND BEYOND: THE CSCE PROCESS IN PERSPECTIVE

edited by

NILS ANDRÉN

and

KARL E. BIRNBAUM

SIJTHOFF & NOORDHOFF 1980
Alphen aan den Rijn, The Netherlands
Rockville, Maryland, USA

Library of Congress Catalog Card Number: 80–53093

ISBN 90 286 0250 X

Printed in The Netherlands

PREFACE

In the 1970s the CSCE "process" has been the chief diplomatic instrument for discussions on security and cooperation among all European states, with the addition of the two North American allies of Western Europe, the United States and Canada. It differs in several respects from all other arenas dealing with matters related to inter-bloc security problems. The pan-European participation is a major characteristic; SALT is largely a superpower affair, while MBFR, as a negotiation process, is limited to the powers in the area where it is hoped to effect multilateral force reductions. Further, the CSCE deals with a broader range of matters in its three "baskets", the contents of which are of concern to all the participants and, in actual fact, more so to other powers than the two supergrands. Hence the lively and persistent interest in the CSCE process not least among the neutral and nonaligned (NN) states.

The CSCE process fascinates participants, observers and analysts for other reasons too. The consensus rule is not only a symbol of the sovereign equality of its participants but also an indication of the difficulty in producing clearcut decisions on distinctly controversial issues. It is a powerless "organization" with, conceivably, some potential influence. In the CSCE the nominal equality of thirty-five states is reflected in an equitable diplomatic practice with more than symbolic significance. The outcome of this attempt to "democratize" international politics seems uncertain: however, there can be no doubt that particularly the smaller European states look upon the CSCE as an instrument for a wider diffusion of influence in international politics. This serves to underline the vested interest of these states in the continuity and viability of the CSCE process. But the "equality among unequals" adds to the difficulty of enhancing the political influence of the CSCE process.

In the present volume the reader's attention is focused on the superpowers and on three distinct groups of states: the nine member states of the European Community, the member states of WTO and the neutral and nonaligned states. This design may be open to the objection that it dwarfs the contribution of individual states other than the superpowers, e.g., Norway and Spain who both played a very active role in Helsinki, Geneva and Belgrade. Yet, on balance, the selected design reflects the predominant pattern of the CSCE negotiations. In these negotiations between thirty-five individual governments, the most important bargains were struck between the main actors mentioned: the superpowers, the "mighty Nine" – as the European Community countries were called by a prominent Soviet diplomat – and the NN group.

The first part of the volume includes the revised version of papers discussed at a seminar* organized by the Swedish Institute of International Affairs in June 1978 to assess the results of the first CSCE follow-up meeting in Belgrade 1977. The second part of the book consists of contributions analysing the CSCE process as a whole, in the light of long-term developments, including the CSCE negotiations in Helsinki, Geneva and Belgrade as well as subsequent expert meetings convened after Belgrade. While none of the latter signified particularly important developments in East-West relations, they all form part of a comprehensive process of multilateral negotiations that will reach a crucial stage with the forthcoming follow-up meeting in Madrid in late 1980. Hence the concluding documentary section comprises not only documents from the Belgrade meeting but also the reports from three meetings of experts convened in 1978–79: the Bonn Meeting on a Scientific Forum, June–July 1978, the Montreux meeting on the Peaceful Settlement of Disputes, October–December 1978 and the Valletta Meeting on Mediterranean Problems, February–March 1979.

One final but obvious observation. This book was both conceived and completed long before the current crises in Iran and Afghanistan. Since the Belgrade conference much has happened to the international relationships constituting the pattern of détente. Its

*A special grant from the Fritz Thyssen Stiftung, which provided essential funding for this seminar, is gratefully acknowledged.

prospects are today obscured by grave controversy. But the necessity of a dialogue between East and West remains. The present volume is published in the belief that the CSCE process may still prove useful for keeping distrust between East and West in Europe on a manageable level and, hopefully, also for promoting a more genuine community of interest.

Nils Andrén Karl E. Birnbaum

TABLE OF CONTENTS

LIST OF CONTRIBUTORS

Prof. Frans A.M. Alting von Geusau, Director, John F. Kennedy Institute, Tilburg University, The Netherlands

Prof. Nils Andrén, Head of the Division for International Studies of the National Defence Research Institute, Sweden

Prof. Karl E. Birnbaum, Director, Austrian Institute for International Affairs

Mr. Richard Davy, The Times, London

Prof. Curt Gasteyger, Graduate Institute of International Studies, Geneva

Prof. Leo Mates, Belgrade

Dr. Jerzy Nowak, Ministry of Foreign Affairs, Warsaw

Mr. Luigi Valsalice, Italian Diplomat, Rome

Part I

GOALS AND EXPECTATIONS

Chapter 1

THE UNITED STATES

by *Richard Davy*

The United States has been widely criticized for the way it approached the Belgrade meeting. In East and West and among neutrals and the non-aligned it is accused of having used the conference as a platform from which to demonstrate its commitment to human rights, thereby unnecessarily provoking the Russians, heightening tension, worsening the situation of human rights activists in the Warsaw Pact countries, and making it impossible for the meeting to agree on practical proposals for following up the Final Act of the Helsinki Conference. Its critics saddle it with a substantial share of the blame for the fact that the meeting fulfilled only part of the mandate agreed at Helsinki. Although the participating states exchanged views on implementation, they made no progress towards "the deepening of their mutual relations, the improvement of security and the development of cooperation in Europe, and the development of the process of détente in the future". Mr. Don Cook set out the indictment in an article entitled "Making the Americans Look Foolish" in the *Saturday Review* of May 5th, 1978:

> Goldberg and the American delegation adopted tactics that played straight into the Russians' hands. According to the ruling political fixation, the conference had to produce a statement of some kind on human rights, and if the Russians wouldn't agree to such a statement, it would be better to settle for nothing. What Goldberg never seemed to grasp was that "nothing" was just fine with the Russians. Moreover, the American position effectively denied the West any room for manoeuvre during the whole twenty-week conference – leaving a residue of bitterness among the Europeans.

In order to examine these criticisms it is necessary to go back and recognize that ever since the start of the CSCE negotiations the priorities and perceptions of the United States have differed from those of the Europeans. Dr. Kissinger was contemptuous of the whole enterprise in the early stages. It did not fit his concept of a European order guaranteed primarily by the mutual security interests of the great powers. Indeed it formally endorsed the somewhat unrealistic notion that Europe consists of equal and sovereign nations. Furthermore it postulated societal change as a condition of détente, a concept from which Dr. Kissinger had been doing his best to wean the United States. Beyond this it also threatened to raise expectations which might be destabilising.

Of course this did not stop Dr. Kissinger from slowly realising that he could use the Soviet Union's desire for a security conference as a bargaining lever. He used it to help buy the West German-Soviet Agreement, the Quadripartite Agreement on Berlin and the MBFR Talks. And in the end, when Dr. Kissinger woke up to the seriousness of the European purpose, he used his personal influence with Mr. Gromyko to get the Soviet Union to accept the Basket 3 Draft which had been negotiated in Geneva. But he never showed any signs of seeing intrinsic value in the conference itself and seemed wholly uninterested in negotiations on human rights, human contacts and other humanitarian proposals.

During the Presidential election campaign of 1976 American perceptions became further clouded. Dr. Kissinger's critics on the Right were very anxious to label him soft on Communism. Therefore they spread the wholly false notion that the Helsinki Conference represented a Soviet victory and an American recognition of the status quo in Europe, including Soviet hegemony over Eastern Europe. In the over-heated atmosphere of the campaign, and with the credibility of the Ford Administration crumbling, Dr. Kissinger's efforts to put the record straight went unheard. This was a surprising failure of communication, but he helped bring it on himself by indicating that where security and justice conflicted in a political settlement he would give preference to security.

With the arrival of the Carter Administration the pendulum of political and public opinion swung towards a new and opposite set of errors. The Final Act was suddenly discovered to be not a betrayal but a weapon in the new campaign for human rights. The hardliners who had attacked President Ford for signing the Final

Act suddenly became the most fervent advocates of its implementation. Newspapers began to refer to the "Helsinki Human Rights Declaration" as if the Final Act had no other content. Monitoring groups, numbering in the end about a hundred, began to spring up. The Commission on Security and Cooperation in Europe, an independent advisory agency drawn from Congress and the Administration, which had been set up under President Ford in the summer of 1976, got its enquiries under way in November and announced with surprise that it found some good in the Final Act after all. By January 1977 its hearings were in full swing and it eventually printed five volumes of testimony. If its approach was not totally even-handed, this was because its mandate was to monitor implementation "with particular regard to the provisions relating to cooperation in humanitarian fields."

With these pressures building up it is not surprising that as the Belgrade meeting approached, the Administration found itself trying to reconcile three conflicting considerations. Firstly, President Carter had to show that he was not retreating from his commitment to human rights. The Press had been sensitised to the issue and was watching him sharply for any signs of back-sliding. It had already noticed a retreat from the more theatrical gestures of the early days of the Administration and was watching Belgrade as a barometer on this issue.

Secondly, President Carter had to avoid further rocking the Western Alliance, some members of which had become very nervous about his human rights campaign. The West Germans were particularly worried about their delicate contacts with East Germany and their efforts to get ethnic Germans out of Poland and the Soviet Union. They and other Europeans felt that the American human rights campaign was determined too much by domestic political considerations and too little by any clear idea of how to get practical results in Europe. In particular they felt the Americans were putting too much emphasis on Soviet dissidents whereas the basic purpose of the CSCE had been to open up human contacts between east and west Europe.

Thirdly, President Carter had to avoid further damage to his bilateral relations with the Soviet Union. He had dropped the concept of linkage in the hope that he could gain the freedom to speak out on human rights while continuing to negotiate on arms control and other matters with the Soviet Union. The Soviet Union was not quite so keen on dropping this kind of linkage. It uttered regular warnings that the human rights campaign was poisoning the atmosphere and damaging prospects for negotiation in other areas.

These three considerations were practically impossible to reconcile. If President Carter tried to extract the full political benefit from Belgrade as a platform from which to proclaim his dedication to human rights, he would risk further damaging his relations with the Soviet Union. He was also liable to upset east and west Europe, which would feel the direct effects of Soviet disapproval, especially if this were expressed in the form of curtailing contacts. If, on the other hand, he gave priority to relations with the Soviet Union, he would immediately be seen by his domestic audience as returning to Kissingerism. This might be seen in Europe as another kind of betrayal in that he would be putting super power relations before a genuine concern with the development of human contacts in Europe; but if he then went along with the European preference for quiet diplomacy and practical results, he would be savaged by press and public opinion at home.

His problems were compounded by his inexperience in European affairs and by the ignorance of some American journalists who went to Belgrade with little more than one idea in their minds, which was to watch the American delegation for signs of weakening resolve on human rights and to wait for the moment when the names of Soviet dissidents would be mentioned in plenary sessions of the meeting. There were also more concrete problems in preparing for the meeting. The State Department made no attempt to start negotiating new proposals with the Russians before the meeting because it feared being accused of "collusion". It embarked on the meeting with no clear plan and gradually found that it had been preparing for a different meeting. It had expected the Russians to engage in a much more direct debate on human rights instead of riding out most of the criticism.

At the preliminary procedural talks in Belgrade in the summer, no special problems arose. The United States played a fairly low-key role. It went along with the Nine on most points, though in the early stages it took a tougher stand on the need for an open-ended conference. Mr. Sherer, then head of the delegation, called a press conference to say that he would rather not have a target date for ending the conference. The paper tabled by the West was, he said, a workable compromise between different points of view.

In the closing phases of the preparatory talks the roles were partly reversed. Agreement had been reached on a formula which seemed to assure a satisfactory review of implementation. Since this was what mattered most to the Americans they became ready to compromise on termination procedure. The West Germans were also ready to compromise, but the French, the Dutch and above all the British, held out for an open-ended conference and achieved it. This difference served to emphasise again that the United States was more interested in the review of implementation while Europeans still hoped for agreement on practical proposals.

When the main meeting started in Belgrade in the autumn, the conflicting pressures on the United States became more apparent. Indeed they were built into the American delegation by its curious composition. In the words of the President's third semi-annual report, it included "all of the Congressional members of the CSCE Commission as well as members of the Commission staff, a number of distinguished public members from business, academia, the labour movement, and other walks of life, plus representatives of several Government departments and agencies, including the departments of State, Commerce and Defense. In preparing for the Belgrade Conference the United States delegation called upon the resources of other government departments and, with the assistance of the CSCE Commission, heard the views of numerous private organisations whose interests are affected by the provisions of the Final Act". Many of these latter were ethnic and other groups interested primarily in human rights.

More significant still was the appointment of Mr. Arthur Goldberg as head of the delegation. With his proven commitment to human rights and his experience of facing the Russians in the United Nations, he seemed ideal from the political point of view. But his appointment was not without controversy. Some sections of the American press decided that Mr. Goldberg was appointed to cover up the President's assumed retreat from his commitment to human rights. Others saw the appointment as intended primarily to counteract the more cautious and alliance-orientated attitude of the State Department. As a result, Mr. Goldberg found himself being criticised from several different directions – sometimes for not being firm enough on human rights and sometimes for causing unnecessary trouble by being too provocative – for instance by mentioning the names of dissidents or accusing named countries of specific violations of the Final Act.

Mr. Goldberg clearly saw himself as the President's personal envoy. He told journalists in Belgrade that he had no specific instructions from the President, and indeed he pursued his task with every sign of having wide latitude. But there were conflicting pressures on him. On the one hand he had to give high priority to upholding the Presidential commitment to human rights in the eyes of the American Press and public. On the other hand he realised that he could not use the meeting only as a platform from which to attack the Russians. In the hope of reducing bitterness, he attempted to establish warm and personal relations with Mr. Vorontsov, the head of the Soviet delegation, but the diplomatic results of his efforts were limited. Meanwhile the State Department was not happy. Apart from having its own man, Mr. Sherer, subordinated to a political appointee, it was acutely aware of the feelings of other members of the Western Alliance, and it very naturally tended to give higher priority to these feelings than to the public image of the President. Its own assessment of the meeting had been set out in very balanced detail by Mr. Matthew Nimetz, who emphasised that the meeting would deal with the full range of East-West issues – political, military, economic, humanitarian and cultural. The United States, he said, wished to use the meeting to develop the promise of *all* aspects of the Final Act. He gave a prominent place to human rights, saying that the President believed that the CSCE should contribute to elevating international standards affecting the treatment of people by governments, but he put this firmly in the European context, emphasising the need to encourage "more normal relations between the West and the peoples and governments of Eastern Europe." The United States, he said, attached great importance to the Belgrade meeting and "even greater importance to the entire process of bilateral and multi-lateral interaction which developed out of the Conference on Security and Cooperation in Europe. . . . We seek no confrontation in Belgrade and have no wish to burden other aspects of the East-West relationship."

Mr. Goldberg also arrived in Belgrade insisting that there would be no confrontation, but he was committed to a full and frank review of implementation, so that some confrontation was unavoidable. He was also under pressure from personal friends involved in human rights activities. In his opening speech he tried to combine reconciliation with criticism. He started by saying that the meeting was "one part of the broader process of reducing the risks of confrontation in Europe and of replacing them with opportunities for cooperation . . . the pursuit of human rights does not put détente in jeopardy. Rather it can strengthen détente and provide a further basis for both security and cooperation."

But after a moderate review of implementation in which he noted progress but said it was insufficient, he gave the hungry domestic lions their meat with a trick which annoyed the Russians and worried some Allies. Ostensibly keeping to Alliance policy, he avoided mentioning names of individuals or countries in his speech. He referred only in general terms to cases such as a research student allowed into an archive for a day and then not allowed back to collect his notes; visas granted to journalists on condition that they avoid certain sources of information and opinion; an "ill and aged husband denied after long years of separation the company of his nearly-blind wife and their daughter." But as soon as his speech was over, his Press Officer gave journalists the names of the people involved and even where possible the page references in the *Report on Implementation by the Commission on Security and Cooperation in Europe.* (For instance the archives incident is on page 162 and the tribulations of the nearly-blind wife, Mrs. Michelson, are described on page 82.)

The practice of giving very detailed briefings continued when the meeting went into ostensibly closed session from the second week onwards. Practically every word was relayed to the press afterwards. The Americans were not alone in this. Many Western countries did the same and so did the Russians when it suited their purpose. But the Americans went furthest and gave most detail, and this was considered by some delegations as a breach of the agreement that the sessions should be closed. Every session was in fact conducted with a sharp eye to public relations. After Mr. Goldberg himself, the first American contribution came from Professor Joyce Hughes, an impressive black legal expert, whose presence was presumably intended to answer Russian accusations of discrimination against blacks and women in the United States. She spoke of violations of the Universal Postal Convention, this time specifically mentioning the Soviet Union and Czechoslovakia – the first names and cases to ruffle the waters of the conference. And then of course she gave a full briefing to the press afterwards.

Thus the American delegation soon found itself out ahead of its allies on the human rights question and Washington began to receive complaints from European allies. In response to these, the State Department cabled Mr. Goldberg asking him not to get too far out of line. Mr. Goldberg could then be encountered stalking the corridors of the conference centre, button-holing journalists to complain that he was being muzzled by his allies. Whether this was an excuse or a genuine complaint is not certain, but it did not prevent some fairly sharp exchanges as the conference developed. The usual pattern was for the United States delegation to make specific criticism of the Soviet Union or Czechoslovakia. Then these countries would accuse the United States of poisoning the atmosphere and interfering in their internal affairs. Thereupon Mr. Goldberg would point out that human rights were a proper subject for discussion under Principle 7 of the Final Act, that Principle 6 on non-intervention was not relevant in this context, and that anyway he welcomed mutual criticism and could not understand why others did not welcome it too.

Among the main themes emphasised by the United States were visa procedures, access to archival material, and the persecution of monitoring groups in the Soviet Union. On 9 October, in a statement to the plenary, Mr. Goldberg mentioned Orlov, Shcharansky and Ginsberg by name. Fully aware of what he was doing, he said that some people had argued that it was better to raise such cases bilaterally rather than at the Belgrade meeting, but the United States had raised these and other cases bilaterally at the highest level without success: "In the spirit of dialogue I simply don't understand why it is said that it is not appropriate to raise such matters here. A full, specific and candid review of the human rights and other provisions of the Final Act is the business of this conference."

The tone of the exchanges gradually grew sharper. On 11 November Mr. Goldberg complained about the pejorative adjectives used by the Soviet Ambassador, such as "political hypocrisy, propagandistic approach, crude, provocative, pseudojuridical." He reiterated that the United States did not regard itself as having a perfect record. When the Soviet Union and Czechoslovakia criticized the United States, Mr. Goldberg noted that the criticisms were drawn from American sources. This illustrated the crucial point that "everyone in our country is free to criticise our deficiencies without being subject to harassment, arrest and imprisonment for doing so."

Differences of emphasis within the United States delegation were not only between Mr. Goldberg and the State Department. From time to time visiting Senators who were nominally members of the delegation would fly in to say their pieces, usually with an eye on their newspapers back home. On 25 November Senator Robert Dole introduced an element of linkage into the discussion, saying:

> There is in my opinion a direct connection between the public perceptions of the integrity of the Helsinki process and the ability of governments in the West to carry on the process of détente. Public trials of political dissidents could have a profound effect on pending or subsequent bilateral and multilateral agreements. Most members of the Congress of the United States believe, in my opinion, that human rights cannot be subordinated to development cooperation and security.

The American delegation continued to be readier than its European allies to mention names, particularly the names of Soviet dissidents. Thus Dr. Sakharov was mentioned on 15 November by Mr. Sol Chaikin, a public member of the delegation. Members of the Ukrainian Monitoring Group, such as Rudenko and Tykhy, were mentioned on 12 December by Mr. Spencer Oliver. The Prague trials, which took place during the meeting, stirred up other members of the Alliance as well. But by the time the meeting ended, Mr. Goldberg had had only very limited success in drawing the Warsaw Pact countries into the kind of frank mutual criticism which he envisaged. They held back, perhaps because every time they ventured criticism of the West, their criticisms were welcomed as the beginning of a true dialogue, a legitimation of Principle 7, and a surrender of their claim that such criticism amounted to interference in internal affairs.

The tone of President Carter's final statement on the meeting was determinedly optimistic but it reflected once again the fact that the United States attached more importance to the review of implementation than to practical proposals for deepening implementation in the future. The United States, he said, in a brief statement which mentioned human rights six times, had achieved its three basic goals. These were a full and frank review of implementation, including a detailed discussion on human rights; the maintenance of unity among allies; and the continuation of the process in two years' time at Madrid. He then regretted the failure to agree on new proposals, but he had not mentioned these among his three basic goals.

In the process of the negotiations there had clearly been some distortion of the original balanced purposes set out by Mr. Vance and his State Department officials. Some of the neutrals and non-aligned were very cross. The Swiss spoke out sharply and there was grumbling about the failure to achieve any progress on confidence-building measures.

Is the criticism justified? Did the American tactics really damage the outcome of the Meeting? It is difficult to go back and prove what could have happened if the Americans had adopted a low-key diplomatic approach. President Carter would have certainly come in for very heavy criticism at home and in order to answer this criticism he would have had to produce some very convincing concrete results from Belgrade. If there had been a clear prospect of doing so, if the Russians had given advance hints of practical proposals to which they were prepared to agree and which would have seriously interested the West, then there would have been a very strong case for defying domestic criticism and negotiating quietly for concrete results. But so far there is little evidence that the Soviet Union was prepared for any such progress. The whole thrust of Soviet policy before the meeting was towards limiting damage and warding off criticism. The concrete proposals mentioned by the Soviet Union were mainly intended for political effect and were already known to be unsatisfactory to the West. The Russians showed little interest in CBMs, and spoke mainly of disarmament, which was not the main business of the Meeting. Perhaps if the Americans had tried seriously to pre-negotiate some practical proposals before the meeting opened, the results would have been different; but apart from the fear of appearing to collude with the Russians, which has already been mentioned, there was also a feeling in Washington that the main emphasis at this stage should be on the validity of the Final Act itself rather than on new proposals which might divert attention from it. The review of implementation was therefore emphasized not only as an opportunity to talk about human rights but also in order to keep the entire Final Act at the centre of the stage.

Moreover it can be said in favour of the Americans that the presentation of the human rights issue was not as one-sidely didactic as is sometimes made out. The re-introduction of the moral element into American policy has included a far greater element of self-criticism than in the past. Mr. Goldberg repeatedly emphasized that he was not depicting the United States as without fault or as having fully implemented the Final Act. He pointed out that the United States had been forced into improving its performance, notably by removing restrictions on travel abroad by American citizens and in relaxing requirements for entry visas so that visitors to the United States "will not be excluded because of political affiliation or belief except in the rarest instances." Mr. Goldberg pleaded for mutual admission of shortcomings and mutual criticism, but even this seemed too much for the Warsaw Pact countries. Offered a blank cheque for criticising the United States, they held back for fear of exposing themselves to more criticism from the West. Thus it was not only the aggressiveness of the United States but also the vulnerability of the Warsaw Pact which stood in the way of progress. Real dialogue proved impossible.

What can be said, of course, is that the American emphasis on human rights and particularly on the persecution of monitoring groups in the Soviet Union, made it easier for the Russians to blame the meagre results of the Meeting on the United States. Thus Mr. Vladimir Kravtsov wrote in *New Times*:

> As is well known it was primarily the United States delegation that tried to place narrow, self-seeking and often purely internal political considerations above businesslike cooperation . . . the idea was to mount in Belgrade a massive psychological attack against the Socialist countries and to revise the Final Act so as to legalise interference in their internal affairs.

According to Mr. Kravtsov this complicated the work of the Meeting "making it physically impossible with so much time wasted on polemics to examine many of the issues the Meeting should have taken up."

Thus there are two basic criticisms of the American approach which can be made to stick. Firstly, although there would have been only a slight chance of results, it might have been worth testing the opportunities for starting negotiation of practical proposals before the meeting. This will in fact be done before the Madrid meeting. Secondly, distorted perceptions of the American press and public meant that disproportionate emphasis was put on Soviet dissidents and internal Soviet violations of the Final Act. This had two effects: It gave the Russians an excuse for obduracy, and it obscured the primary purpose of the Final Act, which was to open up contacts between east and west Europe in the hope of contributing to security by alleviating the tensions deriving from the human, cultural and economic division of the continent. As a result, the United States lost sympathy among some west Europeans, neutrals and the non-aligned. But whether better results could have been achieved if the Americans had been more sensitive to this area of opinion is still difficult to prove. Without this proof the Americans cannot be held responsible for the meagre outcome of the meeting.

It is also difficult to sustain the case made by some conservatives, and in particular by some Soviet emigrés, that a still tougher line would have produced better results. The West had very little with which to negotiate. During the Geneva negotiations which preceded Helsinki, the Western Alliance could buy concessions because the Soviet Union was deeply committed to holding a security conference. In Belgrade the West had far less bargaining power. A still tougher line would therefore have achieved very little, and if it had been pushed to the point of causing a breakdown of the meeting, there would have been no agreement on a further follow-up in Madrid. This would have brought the entire CSCE process to a standstill, thereby depriving the West of the leverage inherent in the Final Act itself, and very probably ruling out any further progress at all.

Chapter 2

THE NINE AND DÉTENTE

by *Frans A.M. Alting von Geusau**

The nine Member States of the European Communities entered the Belgrade Conference in 1977 with broadly similar goals and expectations as the non-aligned, neutral and other West European countries. According to them the Conference should proceed to an overall review of the implementation of the Final Act of Helsinki, while avoiding rocking the process of détente by East-West recriminations and accusations. They hoped to obtain agreement on a number of additional and limited steps to further détente and cooperation. Finally, they agreed – much more easily than had been the case in Geneva – with the emerging consensus to continue the process of review and discussion, during and after the Belgrade Conference.

Despite these modest goals and equally modest expectations, the Concluding Document is seen by them as a particularly disappointing one. The review part of the Conference produced sharply "different views", and the stated result of "a thorough exchange of views" could hardly conceal the fact that the exchange had been neither thorough nor fruitful. No agreement was reached on a single additional step. Even the agreement to have follow-up and expert meetings gave little support to the view that détente was still to be seen as a continuous process towards improving relations. Whatever the impact may have been of the American emphasis on human rights, the nine agree that the uncompromisingly negative attitude of the Soviet Union is to be seen as the primary reason for the disappointing outcome of the Conference.

*The author is grateful to the participants in the Post-Belgrade Seminar, held in Stockholm from June 7–9, 1978, for their comments on the first presentation of this paper.

In this chapter, we shall review the positions taken by the nine towards the main issues discussed during the Belgrade Conference as well as their attitudes towards détente after Belgrade. In so doing, it should be borne in mind, that the nine – unlike the United States and the Soviet Union – constitute a "negotiating sub-system" rather than a single actor in CSCE negotiations. The review of the positions taken by the nine therefore will be preceded by a discussion of the way the nine function as a negotiating sub-system.

1. The Nine and the CSCE Process

Whenever the nine Member States participate in comprehensive multilateral negotiations – in particular CSCE – they have agreed to harmonize or coordinate their policies according to: (1) the rules laid down by the treaties instituting the European Communities; and (2) the procedures elaborated since 1969 in the framework of European Political Cooperation (EPC). With respect to the first, articles 113 and 116 of the EEC Treaty are especially relevant. Within the scope of "the common commercial policy" provided for by article 113, the Commission shall conduct negotiations with third countries, according to directives issued by the Council and in consultation with a special intergovernmental Committee. The Council shall conclude the agreements on behalf of the community, to which member states have transferred their commercial policy-making powers. Article 116 EEC, moreover, was applicable to CSCE negotiations on the second basket. For matters outside the scope of article 113, but "of particular interest in regard to the Common Market" Member States shall proceed "only by common action" in multilateral negotiations.

Member States have so far insisted on a restrictive interpretation of the scope of powers transferred to the Community institutions in East-West economic relations. As a consequence the second basket was seen as one for intergovernmental coordination rather than community representation. The Communiqué of the 1972 Paris Summit Conference stated in this respect:

> In order to promote détente in Europe, the conference reaffirmed its determination to follow a common commercial policy towards the countries of Eastern Europe with effect from January 1, 1973; Member

States declared their determination to promote a policy of cooperation, founded on reciprocity, with these countries.

This *policy of cooperation* is, at the present stage, closely linked with the preparation and progress of the conference on security and cooperation in Europe to which the enlarged Community and its Member States are called upon to make a *concerted* and constructive contribution. (emphasis added).

The Paris Summit, as one of the precursors of the European Council since 1974, was in fact the supreme body of the mechanism – separate from the communities – known as EPC.[1] Joint preparations for the talks on European Security and Cooperation, appeared as one of the first items on the agenda of the political committee in 1970.

Since July 1971, coordination among the nine has been taking place with the assistance of two expert-groups: the *Group ad hoc CSCE* for economic aspects (basket two) and the *sub-committee CSCE* (other baskets). The *Group ad hoc* was composed of experts from member governments and the EC Commission. Proposals were prepared jointly and tabled during CSCE by the representative of the government holding the chair in the EC Council of Ministers. In Geneva, officials of the Commission, included in the delegation of the government holding the Council chair, took part in the negotiations on the drafting of the text of the second basket.

The *sub-committee CSCE* was composed of experts from Member States only. Whenever agreement was reached on joint proposals, one of the representatives of the nine tabled them on their behalf. The process of EPC coordination also produced a certain division of tasks among delegations. This division of tasks has become known as the system of file-leaders (*chef de file*). Certain delegations were given first responsibility for reporting, making suggestions, presenting proposals and maintaining contact with third-countries' delegations on specific subjects.

Having outlined the rather complicated procedures by which the nine seek coordinated action, we may now turn to evaluating its significance in the CSCE process.

One of the primary aims for EPC has always been to present a *distinct European identity* in international politics. In the French view, such European identity should be distinct in particular from that of the United States. Both prior to the conclusion of the Final

Act in 1975 and during the Belgrade Follow-Up meeting, the American approach enabled the nine to play a role of their own. Until at least the final stages of CSCE, the American Administration manifested limited interest in the multilateral talks. At the same time, no major disagreements were apparent among the fifteen of NATO, which – had they existed – would have caused divisions among the nine. As a consequence, the nine were in a position both to shape the attitudes of the fifteen and to play a role of their own in the multilateral negotiations themselves. EPC coordination probably was most successful in 1972–73. A full draft-text containing proposals for the agenda and the mandates of CSCE was submitted to the multilateral preparatory talks in January 1973, as prepared in EPC in November 1972 and agreed upon in NATO.

At Belgrade, the American attitude was very different. This time the American delegation showed major interest in having a full review of the implementation of the Final Act. Its primary interest was in reviewing the glaring deficiencies in Soviet and East European implementation of the seventh principle and the third basket.[2] Some of the nine Member States publicly voiced concern about the impact this American approach might have on the Belgrade meeting. Although coordination among the nine functioned rather well at Belgrade, they did not play a distinctly visible role of their own. Three interrelated reasons may be mentioned for the relative irrelevance of the nine as a separate actor: first, the nine – reacting also to domestic pressure – could not avoid placing major emphasis on poor implementation of the third basket by Warsaw Pact members; second, the uncompromisingly negative attitude of the Soviet Union left no room for "mediation" between the two superpowers (even the French failed, when they finally proposed their own compromise draft final document); third, coordination among the NATO fifteen worked well enough in Belgrade to make the role of the nine of secondary importance.

For a "negotiating sub-system" like the nine, CSCE had the distinct advantage of being even more cumbersome a process than EPC coordination. The nine therefore were in a position to coordinate their viewpoints without unduly retarding or upsetting the process of multilateral negotiations.

2. The Issues, particularly, at the Belgrade Meeting

As indicated above, the Nine hoped to achieve two aims at the Belgrade meeting: an over-all review of the implementation of the Final Act, and agreement on a number of limited additional steps to further détente and cooperation.

Among the issues discussed at Belgrade, I shall briefly review the positions of the Nine with respect to the military aspects of détente; Basket 2 (economic cooperation); and the seventh principle and Basket 3 (human rights and humanitarian cooperation).

2.1. The military aspects of détente

The Nine have never been able to coordinate their policies with respect to arms control and arms reductions in Europe. No joint initiatives have so far emerged from them in this field. This is due primarily to the fact that France left the integrated military structure of NATO in 1966 and refused to participate in MBFR negotiations. It equally refused to take part in the ENDC and CCD (until the latter's replacement by a new body in 1978). With respect to MBFR, only the Benelux countries, the Federal Republic and Britain directly took part. Italy and Denmark have a "special status" in the Vienna talks, whereas Ireland is not a member of NATO.

During the Multilateral Preparatory Talks on the CSCE in 1972–73 (MPT) an informal group of smaller countries, Austria, The Netherlands, Spain, Sweden and Yugoslavia proposed to discuss the military aspects of détente and in particular to agree on so-called confidence building measures (CBMs). At the time these proposals met with strong resistance from the larger European states (as well as other NATO members and the Warsaw Pact countries) and especially France. While CBMs had become a major concern of many West European countries during the Geneva stage of the CSCE, they were not a particularly suitable subject for EPC coordination at Belgrade, although the Nine with the exception of France supported a number of detailed proposals designed to expand CBMs.

2.2. *Basket 2*

Coordination among the Nine on economic issues had been advanced further during the MPT and CSCE than in any other field, although a strict distinction was maintained between issues inside or outside the external relations competence of the European Communities (trade policies and industrial cooperation respectively).

At Belgrade a number of detailed proposals were made on behalf of the Nine towards improving economic and commercial cooperation and facilitating business contacts in CMEA countries. These proposals could only be realized in the context of an overall East-West package deal implying some substantive progress in the implementation of the CSCE Final Act. Since such a deal was not achieved at Belgrade, nothing came of these initiatives of the Nine.

2.3. *Principle 7 and Basket 3*

As the participating states began their preparations for Belgrade, it soon became clear that the issue of human rights would become the dominant one both in the review part of the conference and in the efforts to agree on additional steps. At least three reasons may be given for this prominent attention to the issue. First of all, the West had insisted during CSCE on the inclusion of the seventh principle and the third basket in the Final Act, as its condition for yielding to the Soviet demand to recognize the political and territorial status quo in Europe. Unlike the other principles and provisions of the Final Act, these required states to take positive steps rather than merely refraining from certain actions. Secondly, the necessity for review was strongly emphasized by the fact that citizens of the Warsaw Pact countries took action to request their own governments to observe at home what they had adhered to in the Final Act, and to monitor compliance. The acts of repression with which these rightful demands were met served notice that the Warsaw Pact countries had no intention to implement the Final Act. Thirdly, the new emphasis on observance of human rights by the Carter Administration added to the saliency of the issue at the Belgrade Conference. During the summer of 1977 it appeared as if some major West European governments were inclined to distance themselves from the Carter approach to the issue. In July 1977, the French President went as far as agreeing with Brezhnev's concern about the breaking of the code of détente by President Carter.[3] The West German Chancellor had difficulty in suppressing his irritation with the lack of caution shown by the American Administration towards interstate détente. Only the Dutch and the British governments supported the new American policy.

These differences, however, had somewhat faded away by the time the Conference began in October 1977, mainly because of the first two reasons mentioned above. Although public attention focused on the sharp exchanges of views between the Soviet and American delegates, the Nine – jointly and individually – also raised these issues and made various specific proposals towards improving respect for human rights and humanitarian cooperation. Like other Western delegations, the French specifically mentioned human rights violations like repressive measures against individuals or groups, barriers placed on religious freedom, and obstacles surrounding the right to emigrate. The Germans joined with specific proposals of the Nine and the Fifteen, e.g., on the right of individuals to monitor the performance of governments, on discontinuing the jamming of radio-broadcasting, on contacts with representatives of foreign missions, on the re-uniting of families and the distribution of newspapers.

The Nine did indeed coordinate their approaches rather well, but as nothing came of the proposals submitted, it is impossible to tell to what extent their cohesion would have stood the test of the more difficult exercise of agreeing on texts.

3. The Nine and Détente

The coordination which has taken place among the Nine on the CSCE and during the Belgrade negotiations cannot disguise the fact that differences still persist in their overall détente policies and perceptions. France may have given up her illusion that détente is but the first step towards *entente* and *cooperation*. But she persists in seeing détente as a process by which she can assert her autonomy in East-West relations.[4] The Federal Republic of Germany continues to adhere to a cautious policy, so as to facilitate inter-German normalization of relations. Bonn equally continues to favour the "Kissingerian approach" to détente rather than the line taken by the present American Administration. The other West European states still hope to promote easier human contacts and agreements on arms control.

For the short-term future, it may be expected that these differences will diminish and that détente will no longer be a valid subject for presenting a European identity, distinct from the NATO Fifteen. Such a trend – apparent already – is the result of an increasing concern about the policies and détente intentions of the Soviet Union since 1975.

The continuous strengthening of Warsaw Pact forces and Soviet naval activities in the Mediterranean, off the coast of Norway and elsewhere have forced NATO members to improve their defense capabilities.

Soviet policies in Africa, Moscow's new arrogance of power, its increased subversive activities in Western Europe and support for terrorist activities, tend to underpin the officially proclaimed definition of détente as a process towards the victory of "socialism". It is a far cry from the Western concept of détente as a political context conducive to reconciliation, accommodation and cooperation.

The recent trials of Soviet human rights activists serve sharp notice that the Kremlin no longer intends to live up to its 1975 promises. As the ideological lines of division in Europe thus become sharper again, the Nine are increasingly aware that the Soviet Union can be no reliable partner in the further development of détente.

Notes

1. The EPC functions on four levels:
– triennial conferences of Heads of State or government, known as the European Council;
– meetings of the Foreign Ministers, six times a year (or more);
– regular consultations between directors general for political affairs, known as the political committee;

– continuous consultation between diplomatic representatives of the nine with third governments and in international organizations and conferences.

2. *The Belgrade Follow-Up Meeting to the Conference on Security and Cooperation in Europe: A Report and Appraisal.* Commission on Security and Cooperation in Europe and the US Congress. Washington D.C., May 17, 1978.

3. See Alting von Geusau, "Détente After Helsinki". *Yearbook of World Affairs,* 1978.

4. See Fontaine "Détente-Entente-Cooperation", in F. Alting von Geusau (ed.), *Uncertain Détente,* Alphen a/d Rijn: Sijthoff & Noordhoff, 1978.

Chapter 3

THE SOVIET UNION AND BELGRADE

by *Curt Gasteyger*

This contribution proposes to examine three questions:
– Why did the Soviet Union at the Belgrade Conference act the way she did?
– How did this affect the Conference and what consequences may it have for its follow-up?
– What are the general implications for détente and European security?

1. The Soviet Union in a Changed International Environment

Our first contention is that there are few, if any countries participating in the CSCE for which the circumstances under which they came to Belgrade had changed in more ways than the Soviet Union. Compared with the situation at the time of the Helsinki summit meeting in August 1975 the international environment and political climate before and at Belgrade must have looked very different to the Soviet leaders. There are several reasons for this.

1.1. Détente Reappraised

First and perhaps foremost, there was a noticeable cooling-off of détente, a rather farreaching though often undefined reappraisal of its merits and a general decline of expectations connected with it. Paradoxically enough, this was primarily a result of the CSCE itself. It had lasted too long and its results were considered too ambiguous to make it the beginning of a new phase in East-West relations. Instead of pushing the momentum of East-West rapprochement forward, with the prospect of new possibilities and directions, it slowed it down considerably, often to the point of standstill. The solemn consecration of the status quo in Europe became thus not a springboard allowing for more progress but a barrier just strong enough to arrest the erosion of what had been painfully achieved.

In the course of this development the Soviet Union, formerly the main champion of the CSCE *idea,* began to have second thoughts about its *effects* and probably also about its general concept. In her view, she had made considerable concessions to attain what most observers believe was her main objective: a general recognition of the status quo in Europe. However, these same concessions developed their own momentum by precisely putting into question some of the very assumptions this status quo was supposed to rest upon, i.e. non-interference from the outside, and political tranquillity at home — at least within the Soviet sphere of influence.

Moscow's natural reaction to this was defensive if not repressive; whereas the natural (albeit somewhat surprising in its extent) reaction in the West was disenchantment turning either into an indifference towards détente, or an almost aggressive activism in the field of human rights so much neglected or bypassed up to date.

1.2. A New Dimension: Human Rights

The latter was given a major upswing by the arrival of a new administration in the United States under President Carter. In order to regain broader domestic support of a policy of détente in general, and the dialogue with the Soviet Union in particular, Carter laid specific emphasis on the human rights (symbolized by "Basket 3"). Here seemed to be an issue on which the West could find itself not only in a strong position. Rather, it was one on which it could recapture the initiative from the Soviet Union who was thought (probably wrongly) to have gained the upper hand in Helsinki, while at the same time making political mileage at home.

Western insistence on a greater respect for human rights in communist countries implied, overtly or indirectly, a change in their political regimes. As such it made détente once more respectable in the eyes of an increasingly diffident Western (and American) public. Whatever the merits of this concept were or are, it had the ambivalent effect of making détente or, more precisely, the relations with the Soviet Union, as much an issue of domestic politicking as of foreign *Realpolitik.* This was true primarily but by no means exclusively, for the US.

"Domestic" it became in a double and, for the communist countries, a truly double-edged sense: not only did "Basket 3" influence Western attitudes; it also became an issue within these countries themselves. The Soviet Union, who had always addressed herself as much to Western *societies* as to Western *governments,* found to her surprise that with the Final Act, she had given the latter an instrument to do almost the same in reverse. These closed communist societies became for the first time the addressees of Western policy; its targets were (in a limited way) people rather than parties, individuals rather than organized movements. Nothing could have been more alien than this to Soviet officials still deeply imbued with the 19th century tradition that it is the ruling authority alone to which outsiders must turn.

1.3. The Changing International Scene

As if to compensate for its newly challenged vulnerability, the Soviet Union pursued the expansion of her military presence in Eastern Europe and her politico-military involvement, in extra-European areas. The latter is now, for the first time, supported by a corresponding capability for "global reach". To be sure, this growth of military power to imperial or global dimensions is not something of recent date but rather the consequence of many years of sustained and considerable efforts. What made its psychological impact, however, so great (perhaps disproportionate in relation to its actual and lasting effect) was not only that it coincided roughly with American military retrenchment but also that it alarmed Western public opinion precisely at a time when the Soviet Union promoted the CSCE with its attempt at stabilizing inter-bloc relations. This double coincidence created in the West the impression of a major shift in the global balance. Possibly without Soviet intent, it thus changed the overall context within which it approached the new round of East-West negotiations.

The more Moscow moved ahead with its seemingly excessive

armament in Eastern Europe and its intrusion into African affairs, the more its plea for détente became ambivalent, if not implausible (except, of course, if one accepts that the Soviet understanding of détente differs fundamentally from that of the West). It was criticised as "selective" where it applied to specific regions only (primarily Europe) while at the same time other regions were turned into fields of growing competition. It was criticised as "onesided" where it allowed Moscow to advocate political and social change in Western societies while barring its discussion on those of the communist world. Such double ambiguity was bound to generate greater Western insistence on reciprocity in East-West relations in general, and human rights in particular, than it probably would have under conditions of a more relaxed political climate.

At the same time the Soviet leadership found itself confronted not only with a new US Administration but with a President who, as a person, was unpredictable, and as a politician an unknown quantity. It was the kind of combination to make every Soviet leadership doubly distrustful. Moscow must therefore have felt extremely uncomfortable but at the same time tempted to test the President's resilience and determination. The ups and downs in Soviet-American relations have been a fairly true reflection of this mixture ever since Secretary of State Vance's lamentable mission to Moscow in spring 1977. It tends to confirm that the Soviet appraisal of US strength and willpower has changed over the last few years. In the Soviet view the US has become more realistic about the limits of its own power and more reluctant about its use. It has also become more cautious about Soviet politico-military capabilities and hence more hesitant to engage in a new strategic arms race. Carter's decision to cancel the B-1 Bomber production and his waverings about (and later postponement of) the production of the neutron bomb have to be seen in the light of this perception: they may have pleased the Soviets but at the same time they may have confirmed their impression that the President is either indecisive or inexperienced – or both, and hence weak. This might have strengthened the hands of those in the Kremlin who advocate a tougher course. However that may be, a pervading feeling of puzzlement over Carter remains, not just in Western capitals but above all in Moscow. Carter's strong moral commitment to human rights and arms control does not necessarily make him easier to deal with. The prospect to be confronted at Belgrade with a US delegation determined to adopt a high rather than a low profile must have made the Soviet Union even more circumspect than originally intended.

1.4. Changes in Western Europe

Developments on the European scene were, in a way, no less surprising or disturbing. Within a span of only two years (1974–76) the last three authoritarian regimes in Western Europe (Greece, Portugal and Spain) were swept away making it, for the first time in history, a region governed exclusively by democracies. This not only enhanced Western credibility as "bastion" of democracy; it certainly encouraged the West to go to Belgrade with greater assertiveness on issues regarding the respect of human rights and liberties (though the economic crisis with its social consequences cast a shadow on this rosy picture). It also confirmed Western Europe's claim of its capacity for farreaching political reform without repression or collapse.

At the same time, one must assume that what was to be called "Eurocommunism" worried the Soviet leaders as much (though differently and for different reasons) as the United States. Whether or not, and to what extent, the Communist Parties that fall under the very vague heading of "Eurocommunism", became actually "independent" of Moscow matters less in this context than the fact that, for reasons of their own credibility with their respective constituencies they, too, had to take up the human rights issue. Inevitably, they could hardly avoid making some open or veiled criticism of Soviet practices in this field or even the Soviet system as such. Whatever form this criticism took, it must have embarrassed Moscow. Neither Signor Berlinguer's assertion in favour of Italy's remaining in NATO nor Monsieur Marchais' abandoning of the concept of the "dictatorship of the proletariat", let alone Señor Carrillo's direct attack on the Soviet system were apt to make Soviet leaders very confident about the future orientation, reliability and support of these (and like-minded) CPs in Western Europe.

If even formerly loyal friends came up against some aspects of Soviet life this forebode ill for the general climate to expect in Belgrade.

1.5. Indebtedness

To complete this picture one might mention in passing the overall slowing down of East-West trade and the still growing amount of debts that the Comecon countries – though with significant differences – have accumulated over recent years. The trade remained unbalanced both as regards the export-import ratio (usually in favour of the Western countries) and its composition in terms of commodities traded. Neither trend should be overdramatized. Comecon countries are reputed to be "reliable debtors". Also, some of them have made considerable efforts to reverse the balance of trade in their favour or at least reduce the deficit. But in the general climate of Western weariness about détente and wariness about Soviet military build-up, such factors weighed again more heavily than they otherwise might have done. To be more or less discreetly reminded by Western officials or bankers of these debts and the structural deficiencies causing them, dampened Soviet expectations of commercial benefits at Belgrade.

2. The Impact at Belgrade

2.1. Damage Limitation

If these were the general contours of changes and trends in the political environment the Soviet Union found on her way to Belgrade, they help to explain why her attitude stiffened during the conference. It was a mixture of caution and irritation generating unwillingness for concessions over issues that went to the very heart of the Soviet regime.

One can only speculate about the controversies which are going on within the Soviet leadership about the cost-benefit ratio of détente, the risk and advantages of its further pursuit or at least the way it had been conducted so far. If there is one important sign that Breshnev wanted the continuation of détente as embodied in the Final Act it is the formal (though, at the expense of principles I and VII [human rights], somewhat distorted) inclusion of ten principles from the Final Act into the new Soviet constitution, quite an unusual procedure. It can be interpreted as the will to elevate these principles to constitutional prescriptions for Soviet foreign policy. As such they are a signal not only to the outside world but also to potential challengers of détente from the inside.

However this may be, there is sufficient evidence to conclude that Moscow was determined not to let the Belgrade conference become more than a holding operation. Hence, the strategy adopted for Belgrade was one – in strategic jargon – of "damage limitation". It contrasted with the Western strategies which ranged from "massive retaliation" to "assured but graduated criticism". It was, in other words, essentially a strategy emanating from a basically defensive, occasionally baffled attitude. It revealed a small margin of manoeuvre and an evidently limited willingness to go beyond the absolutely unavoidable.

Such attitude left little room for bargaining. It implied, or even accepted, the risk of appearing the major stumbling block to more concrete and positive achievement, of preventing Belgrade from becoming another milestone in a continuously progressing progress, including a review of past insufficiencies and future improvements.

Inevitably, there was a price to be paid for such strategy. The first and most obvious one was a loss of face and credibility as the previously major champion of the CSCE. Part of this price had already been paid when the Soviet Union's interest in the CSCE slackened even before the Final Act came up for signature. A second, less obvious price must have been the genuine unhappiness among most East European countries about Soviet behaviour at Belgrade. They had less to fear on human rights and more to gain in other fields than the Soviet Union. And yet, they had little other choice than to follow suit – with the traditional but hardly more successful exception of Rumania. They were perhaps among those who lost most by this turn of events. And finally, the Soviet Union seems (or claims) to have been willing to concede more to Western Europe had she not feared that this would be interpreted as yielding to American toughness: given the special pressure she was confronted with, this was precisely the impression she wanted to avoid under any circumstances. That is at least what the Soviet delegates wished to convey to their foreign colleagues in the attempt to justify their rigid position. Such tactics acquire relevance where they reflect an acute Soviet perception of differences within the Western camp, and aim at playing one against the other (in this instance, Western Europe against the US). This no doubt happened in Belgrade and has gathered momentum ever since.

However, even if what the Soviet Union tries to insinuate is true, the fact remains that she was hardly in a position to give much. It may be that the West offered too little to allow for a minimum of bargaining. Only very late in the game the West (i.e. above all the European Community) came around to accept reluctantly the Soviet proposals for holding under the auspices of the Economic Commission for Europe a pan-European conference on environment – and even here there was too little substance for a mutual *do ut des*. Contrary, then, to the CSCE proper, there was at Belgrade no or insufficient substance for negotiation: it left the Soviet Union little to trade for. That at least is again the self-serving explanation she offers to explain her rigidity.

2.2. The NN and a Return to the Blocs?

It would be an oversimplification to state that Belgrade has again accentuated the bloc-to-bloc confrontation. But it is probably true that the human rights issue brought into sharper focus the fundamental differences still dividing the two socio-political systems in Europe. It could hardly have been otherwise – and perhaps it was necessary to be reminded of this, however much one may deplore it. Whether and to what extent Belgrade favoured a re-emergence of bloc-politics can be best judged by the role and status of the NN group. It certainly became clearer that they lacked cohesion. This reinforced the impression that their influence had lessened and that they were drawn again into the shadows of bloc-politics.

To what extent this was true at Belgrade is not the subject of the present paper. What is important in our context is the fact that, for all intents and purposes, the Soviet Union was at pains to maintain the cohesion within the communist group and limit whatever margin of action her East European allies had. In this sense the Belgrade conference did not have the effect one might have hoped for: it did not substantially improve or enlarge the manoeuvrability of these countries.

3. Towards Madrid

In the light of what has been said some conclusions – however tentative – can be drawn regarding the future of Soviet détente policy.

First, there is no significant evidence that the Soviet Union does not wish to continue détente in the way practised to date.

Second, Soviet freedom of manoeuver has become substantially limited for the reasons indicated above. This is likely to remain so in the area most sensitive to the Soviet Union, i.e. the protection of human rights in other than the social field. What causes some concern is that too much Western emphasis on this general issue could affect the implementation of the stipulations in Basket 3 where in fact some progress has been made. Soviet freedom of manoeuver is also, though in a different way and less acutely, limited in the economic field.

Third, it is hardly surprising that the Soviet Union places increasing emphasis on initiatives and progress in the field she feels strongest and has most to offer, i.e. the military. A SALT agreement will no doubt be highly relevant, be it for symbolic and psychological reasons only. It can help to relax relations somewhat on the most important level – Soviet-American relations – with favourable repercussions on the other ones. Soviet proposals at Belgrade on other military issues were hardly imaginative and even less acceptable to the West. Little can be expected here though there may be some progress particularly if both the Warsaw Pact countries and the Western side continue what appears to be a more general review of their respective position in the Vienna negotiations on force reduction in Europe.

Fourth, Soviet emphasis on the military dimension of East-West relations has, however, a major drawback: it lends additional (or renewed) importance to the role of military power in East-West relations. In fact, the continued arms build-up and the mutual preoccupation as to how to cope with it, runs counter to a major objective of détente, namely to reduce, in favour of non-military elements, the relevance of military power as the predominant underpinning of stability and security in Europe. The next few years therefore may be decisive as to whether and how the ongoing arms build-up in Europe can be brought under some control, or slowed down.

Fifth, the advent of new, more powerful and precise weapons with greater range will make efforts of arms control even more difficult. This is true for Soviet weapons like the new SS-X-20 as it is for the so-called "Eurostrategic" weapons (e.g., cruise-missiles) to be introduced in the West. They are likely to cause new strains not only between East and West but also within the Western Alliance (i.e. between the US and its European allies). The Soviet Union could feel again tempted to exploit the latter (as she did in the case of the neutron bomb) turning the introduction of such weapons into a moral issue for the West, while using them herself as a pretext to justify her own armament. The victims will be arms control in general, and the dialogue on how to put it into practice in Europe.

Sixth, barring major changes in her political leadership, one can assume that the Soviet Union will not withdraw from the CSCE process or fundamentally alter her policy in it. The alternative would be a renegation, not just of some agreements or procedures adopted in the course of this process. More likely it would put into question the Final Act itself and, in consequence, everything Soviet policy has accomplished with it. This is not to say that there will be no shifts of emphasis and modifications in Soviet attitudes. Thus the commitment to go to Madrid within a relatively short period of time suggests that in spite of considerable misgivings, Moscow has so far shown no sign that would indicate her intention to extricate herself from an increasingly arduous and ambivalent undertaking.

And finally, seventh, the fact that the Soviet Union has become a power with almost global politico-military engagements is bound to render East-West relations (and thus détente) more complex and potentially more vulnerable by adding an extra-European dimension to détente. On the Western side this will increase the temptation to create "linkages" and to judge Soviet behaviour and objectives in Europe (or the East-West context) also by what she is doing outside. Whether or not the West's refusal of "selective détente" is well-founded or inappropriate is immaterial as long as it influences its reaction to Soviet policy in the more narrow East-West context. Conversely, the Soviet Union will find it increasingly difficult to persuade the West that what she is doing outside Europe is prompted by different motives and thus should not be associated with what she is doing in Europe. The Soviet Union will soon discover that she, too, is becoming a prisoner of interdependence.

Chapter 4

AN EAST-EUROPEAN PERSPECTIVE

by *Jerzy Nowak*

1. Context and Expectations

The Belgrade Meeting must be seen in the context of the international situation as a whole and especially of East-West relations. The Meeting was adversely affected by a certain standstill in the process of détente. An intensification of unfortunate military developments; the human rights campaign and the political ends sought through it; the deterioration of relations in Africa and the Middle East – all this reverberated through the proceedings of the Meeting with negative results. Furthermore, it cannot be forgotten that the Belgrade Meeting was only a stage in the process of implementing the CSCE Final Act; it was only a fragment of the multilateral process initiated in Helsinki.

Polish publications preceding the event[1] repeatedly pointed to the fact that the atmosphere created in the West around the Belgrade Meeting was conducive neither to consolidating mutual confidence nor to advancing negotiations. Firstly, the Meeting was ranked in the West almost on a par with the Helsinki Conference, kindling far-reaching hopes entirely out of touch with the reality and the possibilities of the moment. Secondly, the impression was given that the Meeting was supposed to deal exclusively with human rights and selected issues concerning contacts between people and the flow of information.[2] There were voices demanding an evaluation of the socialist countries' behaviour in areas where human rights were involved, as well as attempts to talk those countries into accepting as universal certain Western models, and certain Western solutions of problems touching on human rights and humanitarian issues. By the term "democracy" only the classic solutions of Western parliamentary democracy were understood. One example of this is the so-called Fascell's Report by the US Congress Commission on Security and Cooperation in Europe, published on the eve of the Belgrade Meeting.[3] While evaluating as favourable the practice of publicizing news about the implementation of the Final Act, one should, however, critically note that the cited document dealt with the fulfilment of the Helsinki resolutions not so much by the United States as by other countries, in particular the Soviet Union and other socialist states – and dealt only with selected matters at that. The political bias of the Report could not help to create the atmosphere needed for pragmatic negotiations.

The socialist states of Eastern Europe expected that the Belgrade Meeting would provide a fresh, vital impulse to the process of détente. According to the Warsaw Treaty Committee of Foreign Ministers, the Meeting was called upon to contribute to the strenghthening of mutual understanding and trust among the states and nations and was to be conducted in a constructive way. They also expected that it would furnish the necessary support for the campaign to supplement political détente with military détente. It was only natural to suppose that the Belgrade Meeting would deal with ways and means to improve the implementation of the Final Act. As far as Poland is concerned there was also deep interest in:

– providing an opportunity for the further improvement of relations between states, and marking a step forward in overcoming the division of Europe into two opposed politico-military camps;
– halting the intensifying protectionism in trade, or at least preventing the emergence of new stumbling blocks to trade, industrial cooperation, etc., encouraging the flow of modern technologies, and supporting the idea of holding three all-European congresses on transport, energy and the protection of the natural environment;
– boosting the interest of states in cultural cooperation in order to ensure the enrichment of the value of all national cultures, to consolidate the identity of every state, and to offset unjustified and harmful disproportions in cultural exchanges between states.

In summary, it can be said that the socialist countries placed strong emphasis on a comprehensive development of realistic cooperation.

Worth recalling here are appeals, launched in Poland prior to the Belgrade Meeting, for a down-to-earth approach to cooperation.[4] In the Polish view put forward then, a useful attitude to the Belgrade Meeting would have embraced, among other things:

– the positive shaping of practices in bilateral and multilateral relations; the creation of an auspicious political climate for the development of cooperation; the increasing of the convergence of views on various matters;

– the setting of positive precedents for the implementation of already adopted agreements in individual areas of cooperation, including those where humanitarian ideals are involved;

– exercising moderation and patience so as to prevent the Belgrade Meeting from turning into a forum for making mutual accusations or for drawing up lists of actual or alleged transgressions – meetings of the Belgrade kind should provide occasions for reviewing the positive experiences to date and for charting the directions of cooperation in the future.

Such an attitude is still valid, because it is of a universal character, and as such should apply to the entire process of détente and the development of cooperation. Undoubtedly, there has been no experience of peaceful cooperation lasting long enough to provide a basis for confidence in its usefulness and trust that it does not imply dangers for internal political stability and social order. However, these considerations only add to the urgent need for steps conducive to shaping international relations in a peaceful and far-sighted manner.

2. Differing Approaches: The Failure of Pragmatism

The standpoint represented by Poland and the other socialist countries was confronted in Belgrade by that represented by a majority of the NATO states. It seemed that the Western side was largely trying to reduce the CSCE process to humanitarian concerns alone, to bypass the role played by states and their organs in international relations and cooperation. There was also an effort to legitimize on an international plane the minority opposition and dissidence in socialist countries and to put forward a whole catalogue of unrealistic postulates concerning contacts between people and the flow of information. This is how the Western effort in Belgrade "to give a new emphasis to the human dimension of détente" was interpreted in Eastern Europe.

Nobody denies the significance of the humanitarian side of détente. Ultimately, the strengthening of peace and security and the development of cooperation will assist in the consolidation and extension of human rights for all peoples, not only in Europe but throughout the world. However, it seems there was no need to attach incommensurate importance to one issue – that is, to human rights, especially narrowly interpreted – at the expense of taking into consideration the other principles of the Final Act.

It follows from the course of the Belgrade negotiations that some NATO states were seeking to work out a new "Belgrade version" of the Final Act, a kind of "reader's digest" for the man in the street, which would omit some issues while either spotlighting or soft-pedalling others. Some problems thus approached were the pressing of the human rights issue, the attempts to divide principles into active and passive, the exaggeration of the importance of confidence-building measures with the simultaneous reluctance to give political backing to steps towards disarmament, and the emphasis on direct contacts between individuals without paying due attention to various fields of economic and cultural cooperation. Such endeavours seemed to threaten to push the Final Act into the shadow and eventually into oblivion. In effect, the Polish delegation in Belgrade, like the other delegations from the socialist countries, devoted a significant part of its activity to defending the Final Act, to prevent a disruption of the balance of interests which had been incorporated there.

During the "thorough exchange of views" the socialist countries also expected to hear more from the Western states about what they had done, and what they were going to do in the future, to implement the CSCE Final Act. With slight exceptions, this, regrettably, did not happen. Obviously it was understandable to everybody that the presentation of some difficulties in relations between the CSCE partners could not be avoided. However, one could expect this to be done carefully and tactfully. It turned out that those who thought that the attempts to size up the behaviour of other states would be harmful were right. Such attempts inevitably lead to polemics or downright confrontation, with states taking sides according to their different socio-political systems.

The possibility of interference into internal affairs became an issue as a result of some moves by Western delegations at Belgrade. The East European side interpreted them as attempts to award good or bad marks to individual countries or to bring up all the many outstanding individual cases being pursued through bilateral channels. These attempts led to an ideological and propaganda-type debate, jeopardizing genuine negotiations, obscuring the aims and character of the process initiated at Helsinki. In this situation, with the gap between attitudes widening, while the attitudes themselves were becoming increasingly intransigent, the impossibility of arriving at agreements was a foregone conclusion.

From the Polish viewpoint, it is regrettable that the NATO states did not consent to expanding the concluding document of the Belgrade Meeting with a number of provisions which had been approved by virtually all the participants. The NATO states argued that their basic postulates had not been taken into account. That was true, but one should bear in mind that their proposals were of an unrealistic nature. Furthermore, the fact should be borne in mind that the basic postulates advanced by the socialist states – for example, in the Soviet "Platform of Action with a View to the Consolidation of Military Détente in Europe"[5] – had not been accepted either. Nevertheless the socialist countries did not adopt an "all-or-nothing" attitude. The important point is that the numerous, if sometimes fragmentary, recommendations which had been agreed upon, would have marked some headway, however modest. If not a big stride, at least a short step in the right direction would have been possible. The conclusion to be drawn is that in complex situations one should avoid going to extremes and rest content with the progress that is feasible, that can be accepted by all concerned, at the given moment.

With such an assumption in mind, the Polish delegation to the Belgrade Meeting came out for a reasonable attitude and the adoption of at least "minimal" decisions. Poland's realistic evaluation of the Meeting, the Meeting's tasks and possibilities in the prevailing international circumstances of that time, was sometimes wrongly interpreted by some mass media in Western and neutral countries as an attempt to detract from the importance of the Belgrade event. Such an interpretation is far from true. Poland criticized only the "all-or-nothing" attitude as harmful.

3. The Achievements

The question arises as what role the Belgrade Meeting has played in the détente process. Let us recall that "Belgrade 77" was one of the elements of the comprehensive process of détente initiated at Helsinki. It fulfilled its basic tasks: the representatives of the thirty-five states reaffirmed at Belgrade the resolute will of their governments to implement the Final Act, and agreed upon concrete ways of ensuring the continuity of the CSCE process on a multilateral basis. The Meeting in a way reconfirmed the viability of the Final Act. All its participants, irrespective of the differences dividing them, reaffirmed that the continued détente process is the sole alternative ensuring the strengthening of European security and cooperation. The sentence of the concluding document referring to the proposals which were not approved indicates that the difficulties which had arisen during the Meeting did not diminish the importance which the participant states attach to the CSCE process.

There can be no doubt that many more decisions could have been reached in Belgrade, had it not been for an atmosphere of pressure and ideological confrontation, and for the attempts to exploit the Meeting for ends contravening the letter and spirit of the CSCE resolutions. For this reason, "Belgrade 77" was an education in political realism. It revealed that attempting to legalize interference in the internal affairs of other states and striving to gain unilateral advantages are methods doomed to failure.

The Belgrade Meeting signified a totally new experience in the relations between the thirty-five states: namely, the "thorough exchange of views" on the implementation of the CSCE Final Act. The review stage of the Belgrade Meeting is commonly described in Western publications as "a real success".[6] One can hardly share this opinion. The polemical approach taken by a number of NATO delegations not only endangered the process of the negotiations in Belgrade but also, in some respects, the implementation of the results. However, the exchange of opinion and the review of charges and postulates were useful in some respects. They brought certain insights important for the continuity of the process:

– firstly: the period of two years which had elapsed since the Helsinki Conference was too short a time to properly harmonize cooperation and make a significant step forward on the multilateral level;
– secondly: the participants in the Belgrade Meeting became more familiar with the mechanisms of cooperation as well as the limits of and possibilities for compromise. They might become convinced that bilateral relations between many states having different socio-political systems (for example, between Poland and France, Austria, Sweden) continue to offer large, as yet unused, potentials for cooperation, or even for shaping solution models which in time could be followed by other countries;
– thirdly: the Meeting has revealed the need on the one hand to avoid propaganda-type confrontations in diplomatic negotiations and on the other hand to expand political realism, and at some stage to give up extreme expectations and "wishful thinking". This would favour actual, even though limited progress;
– fourthly: the success of multilateral negotiations of the Belgrade type largely depends on their prior and concrete preparation through bilateral contacts, and on avoiding surprising partners with unrealistic and, sometimes, extreme proposals.

The Belgrade Meeting has failed to give a clear indication of how the difficulties should be overcome, the gaps between the states' priorities narrowed, and the level of their involvement in cooperation adjusted. But it has brought home to everybody the weight and proportions of the problem. Many proposals have been forwarded which constitute valuable material for reflection and implementation. Some of them can serve as guideposts to Madrid.

The Meeting has shown that all-European cooperation, particularly in the context of East-West relations, is developing, though slowly, but encountering various difficulties. The main stumbling blocks are: the differing internal structures and the related differing mechanisms for international cooperation; the divergent national interests and priorities; as well as the varying degrees of involvement in cooperation. The dynamic factors are: the expanding range of objective requirements for economic and cultural development; the growing tendency to view détente and security in terms of cooperation in all areas; as well as the increasing pressure being exerted by international public opinion to accelerate cooperation, exchanges and contacts. The durability of the dividing walls between states with systems differing notably in ideology, does not rule out the possibility of finding mutual spheres of interest, and of mutually adjusting the mechanisms for cooperation to the objective possibilities of East and West.

All in all, the results of the Belgrade Meeting – despite the limited scope of agreement – are evidence that all the participants treat as superior and common values peace, détente and cooperation. The fundamental problem still facing Europe today consists in maintaining the momentum of détente, expanding it through intensified cooperation, and imparting to it a universal and lasting character. The main way of reaching this objective is through strict respect for all the principles and resolutions of the CSCE Final Act, and through their implementation.[7]

4. Prospects after Belgrade

Numerous articles in scholarly journals and the press attest to a widespread search for ways to improve East-West relations, and to develop security and cooperation in Europe. It is particularly important to single out the practical possibilities for taking new steps, and for making progress. All the CSCE participant states are looking for the right answer to the question – What now?

It follows from the views on the Belgrade Meeting outlined above that both before and after Belgrade the main problems of European security remain fundamentally the same. It was not "Belgrade 77" that defined the problems of and perspectives for the amelioration of the European situation. Rather, a whole complex of political, ideological, social, economic, diplomatic and military factors had a decisive bearing on the Meeting, and its results. These factors have remained fundamentally unchanged.

At present we are facing a loss of momentum in the process of détente. However, there is still much energy to be mined out of a number of significant agreements concluded in Europe at the outset of the 1970's. In the near future it will seem necessary to adopt a proper psychological approach, to deal with less spectacular issues and to take smaller, but qualitatively effective steps forward. There are many opportunities for building, in various areas, infrastructures on which it would later be possible to make meaningful progress.

The most difficult problem is the arms race, which has been intensifying in recent years. The importance of making progress towards halting the arms race does not mean waiting for progress towards achieving military détente. As the peaceful fabric of international relations is woven and the détente process is advanced, cooperation grows markedly in rank and significance. Cooperation constitutes, alongside security, an increasingly important factor in the shaping of a new European system.

Irrespective of persisting ideological and socio-political differences, the emergence of a system of interdependencies should itself constitute a security factor as important as military guarantees. To achieve such a system, to achieve cooperation, it is necessary, *inter alia*:

– to search more intensively, while at the same time observing the rules established in the CSCE Final Act, for ways of reducing the forms and range of conflicts, and the rivalry occurring in contacts and exchanges; to further institutionalize the various forms of governmental and non-governmental consultations and discussions, and to increase their substance;
– to develop forms of cooperation based on long-range agreements wherever possible, to search vigorously for ways of improving the mechanisms for cooperation;
– to strive to achieve objectives by diplomatic means, not by propaganda; to conduct matter-of-fact negotiations; to adopt for such negotiations attitudes of moderation and patience; to avoid attempting to impose one's own solutions on others;

– to apply a maximalist's, not a minimalist's, interpretation of the range and depth of ties created by finalized agreements, including the appropriate recommendations of the CSCE Final Act.

The largest question mark looming on the horizon ahead is how the NATO countries will pursue their policy on human rights. This aspect of their policy is viewed in the East as an attempt from the outside to bring about changes in the social and political structures of Eastern countries. There is no doubt that the obligations set down in international laws, including the Final Act, should be meticulously observed and thoroughly implemented. But this is part of a larger process: normalizing the situation in Europe and developing good relations between countries with different political systems will expand the range of human rights and their observance. Mounting tension in international relations only shrinks liberties.

There is a growing demand for scientific assistance in the shaping of a new system of security and cooperation, for taking a new significant step forward. It can be noted that the spectacular moves in East-West relations at the beginning of this decade rested on very solid intellectual ground which had been laid gradually over many years. It seems that we are now approaching the threshold of a period when new moves in building East-West relations and in shaping an all-European security system will have to be based on new equally solid scientific grounds.

5. Looking forward to Madrid

It would, of course, be of great importance if the Madrid Meeting contributed to the consolidation of a peaceful European structure as a basis for a new move forward in East-West relations. Such meetings should observe certain tested rules characteristic of successful diplomatic conferences and negotiations: respect for the sovereign equality of the partners and a generally constructive approach; taking into consideration not only one's own interests but also those of *all* other participants, and, needless to say, tact and courtesy, which are very helpful on such occasions.[8] Prior to the Meeting, the proposals to be tabled in Madrid should be the subject of bilateral consultations which could develop into a kind of all-European dialogue on the basis of the Belgrade experience. It is also advisable that the proposals are not too numerous.

The Madrid Meeting could adopt the organizational framework worked out at the Preparatory Meeting in Belgrade. However, it is important that the emphasis be put on negotiations. Another significant issue is the question of consensus, not as a way of exerting pressure by one participant on all the others but rather as a means to work out a reasonable compromise. Otherwise the negotiations could stumble on issues linked with some insoluble problems. Adequate concern should be given to the problem of the level of representation during the Madrid Meeting. A "political" level could perhaps facilitate better preparation, a matter-of-fact approach and a smoother process of decision making. But, of course, one should be aware that a decision concerning this question would depend on the actual state and climate of international relations on the eve of the Meeting.

6. Conclusion

Summing up the foregoing thoughts, which are partly of a postulative nature, one could say that despite the existing differences in respect to policies of cooperation, the process of mutual understanding and rapprochement shows an enduring tendency. Very relevant to the prospects for the amelioration of the situation in Europe are two points.

Firstly, the foundations of the security and cooperation system, notably the principles agreed upon in Helsinki, which must be generally recognized.

Secondly, the political and legal framework for cooperation, negotiated in bilateral and multilateral relations, which should be constructively interpreted and honestly implemented. The concept of achieving broad, bold cooperation aimed at achieving equal participation by all in the international division of labour, at achieving equal levels of development of all the partners, and at bringing the cooperating societies closer together in general is superior to the concepts of gaining short-term advantages and of treating the partners from different systems only as of marginal importance, to be discriminated against when economic or political indices show a downward trend. Important instruments for achieving these aims are the creative implementation of the CSCE Final Act and steps to bring about military détente. They would seem to be in accord with both the most vital national interests of Poland and the most vital common interests of Europe as a whole.

Notes

1. For example: Marian Dobrosielski, "Belgrad 1977 – szanse i dylematy", *Nowe Drogi,* no. 9, 1977, pp. 129–140.

2. For example: *Report on Cooperation in Humanitarian and other Fields – Implementation of the Final Act of the CSCE.* Council of Europe, Parliamentary Assembly, Doc. no. 3957 of 31.3.1977.

3. *Implementation of the Final Act of the Conference in Security and Cooperation in Europe: Findings and Recommendations Two Years after Helsinki.* Report by the Commission on Security and Cooperation in Europe. Washington 1977.

4. For example, R. Baturo, "Odprężenie międzynarodowe: przesłanki i treści", *Nowe Drogi,* no. 4, 1976, p. 163 and Jerzy M. Nowak, "East-West Cooperation in Humanitarian Fields After the CSCE", *Studies on International Relations,* no. 8, 1977, p. 75.

5. Proposal of the Soviet Union, no. CSCE/BM/5 of 24 October, 1977.

6. Tessa Solesby, "Helsinki to Belgrade – and Beyond", *NATO Review,* no. 3, June 1978, p. 19.

7. For further information on the Polish evaluation of the Belgrade Meeting see special number of the monthly *Sprawy Międzynarodowe* no. 6, 1978.

8. These ideas are taken from Marian Dobrosielski: *Belgrad 77,* Warsaw, 1978.

Chapter 5

THE NEUTRAL AND NONALIGNED COUNTRIES*

by *Leo Mates*

This paper deals with the goals and expectations of the group of Neutral and Nonaligned (NN) countries in Europe. This group is heterogenous in many respects. Sweden, Switzerland, Finland and Austria form the "Neutrals"; the "Nonaligned" countries are Yugoslavia, Malta and Cyprus. Finally the NN group also includes Liechtenstein and San Marino. There are substantial ideological, political and economic differences between them. They are situated in different parts of the continent and have problems and affinities in their neighbourhoods, which vary greatly from country to country.

These countries established themselves as an identifiable group during the Conference of Helsinki (CSCE). In the bloc polarisation of the Conference – and of European politics – they wished to stay outside not only the two alliances, but also other organizations or groupings. In a way, they had initially a negative common denominator. This is spelled out also in the name of the group (NN) which is in fact an aggregate of two Negatives. Hence, the special status of the nine countries emerged out of the constellation of the Conference, reflecting the political state of relations in Europe. Regardless of separate outside efforts, the Conference came into being as a result of negotiations between East and West.

The original proposals of the Soviet Union were rejected by the West. The general situation made a meaningful debate on all open questions practically impossible. Then, one of the main objectives of the East materialized in the agreements on Berlin and the two

*An abridged version of this paper was presented to the Stockholm seminar, 1978.

Germanies, including the boundary with Poland. The spirit of a European détente prepared the ground for the Conference. But exactly this prehistory and the pattern of relations prevailing in Europe made the NN group necessary as a form for insisting on multilateralism in negotiations and arrangements, as against bilateral bloc relations. In other words, the fundamental ideal uniting the group was and still is the hope of a gradual melting away of the two alliances and of substituting multilateral relations for the prevailing bipolar pattern.

The two alliances were not inclined to go beyond vague and general statements. However, they did (and still do) everything to maintain and reinforce the alliances. They have very little common ground beyond this general idea. Hence, the situation is characterized both by the East-West controversy and by disagreement on the framework of intra-European cooperation – interbloc *versus* multilateral relations.

The role of the NN group in the CSCE process was dual: acting in the two complementary roles of mediators and of constructive independent actors in the East-West controversy, working for dissolving the antagonistic, bipolar pattern. By and large, the mediating role was subordinated to the more ambitious goal of dissolving or, to begin with, reducing the rigidity of the bipolar pattern. A condition for success was a sufficient self-confidence prevailing in the existing bloc structures.

In their work for a multilateral pattern of relations in Europe, the NN countries hence had to recognize that the existing alliances were the only possible framework for the détente, at least in its earlier stages. Thus their goals and aspirations could be presented also as favouring a process with several stages; firstly to strengthen and widen the détente as a relationship which develops mainly along interbloc lines. This should improve the general atmosphere and make it possible gradually to develop more flexibility and more direct state to state relations even across the dividing line separating the two blocs. Ultimately, the process would be expected to affect the basic bipolar pattern itself.

This vision of the desirable course of developments in Europe emerged gradually, mostly after Helsinki, and became more clearly discernible only in Belgrade. But even there it was by no means equally present in the actions of all the actors from the NN group to which, in view of its heterogeneity, it would be futile to ascribe unity of vision and aspirations as a whole. Nevertheless, they preserved, and even strengthened their cooperation and similarity of views in the course of the negotiation. Already in Geneva the NN group had expressed great interest in the follow-up process after Helsinki. This view was subsequently reinforced and became a strongly defended position both in the Preparatory Meeting in Belgrade in June and July 1977 and in the main Belgrade Meeting. This position was derived from the general longterm goal and aspiration in the context of détente in Europe. In order to favour the continuation of the debates started in Helsinki, and to maintain a favourable atmosphere of détente, frequent meetings after the Helsinki Conference were indispensable. They were envisaged both as special expert meetings and as general meetings of government representatives.

Formulating precise statements by participating states on the follow-up process remained a main objective for the Belgrade Meeting. Furthermore, the follow-up process was to be not only precisely defined but from the very outset conceived as an automatic and selfsustained development over many years, covering an unlimited number of meetings. Hence, the NN group resisted all proposals in the Preparatory Meeting in Belgrade aimed at playing down the importance or the time-perspective of the follow-up process. They were opposed to attempts and suggestions of fixing only the next general meeting, i.e. the Madrid conference in 1980.

As to the conditions for the discussions, the Belgrade Meeting was fundamentally different from the Helsinki phase; in Belgrade, the Helsinki Final Act provided a basis and there was an understanding not to change its precarious balance. Helsinki was the creative stage of the process, starting from a vaguely defined concept of détente; in Belgrade the concept was already spelled out. On the other hand, the NN group was not satisfied with an attitude of rejecting any idea of further development. This would be contrary to their basic concept of the process. They wanted to give a dynamic life of its own to the Helsinki Final Act, while preserving the essential harmony and balance which they had helped to insert.

Consequently, the major preoccupation in Belgrade was to preserve the momentum of change, as far as compatible with the need for an atmosphere conducive to change. As a result the proposals submitted by the NN group were modest, mainly aiming at enhancing the confidence-building measures of the Final Act. Other items included in particular the Mediterranean questions, with Malta as the main moving spirit. This also included the continuation of a dialogue with non-participating Mediterranean states.

The NN countries were also greatly preoccupied with the controversy on human rights, opened already in 1976 and continuing practically to the opening of the Belgrade Meeting. Two issues emerged as particularly important. The first concerned the measure for compliance with the human rights principle. It was emphasized that the yardstick for criticism must not be imposed by one side but was represented only by undertaking in the Final Act of Helsinki. The second was the participation in the criticism by the Western Communist Parties, leaving the Soviet Union and other Warsaw Pact countries in a doubly embarrassing position.

The NN countries feared the danger inherent in explosive polemics; at the same time they could not take a condoning attitude in view of the great importance they themselves attached to this issue. They had all supported the inclusion of the human rights issue and the specific formulations in the Final Act. There was no difference of views among them on this issue. The NN group position was greatly facilitated by the moderate position of the Western European states in preparing for the Belgrade meeting which made it easier for the group to define its tactics for Belgrade. Practically speaking, the issue was subordinated to the goals and aspirations as described earlier. The aim was to safeguard the process and, most directly, to save the Belgrade Meeting from breakdown.

Summarizing the basic goals and expectations in preparing for the Belgrade Meeting, the NN group approached the meeting with modest proposals aimed at carrying further the Helsinki agreement and at guaranteeing the continuity of the debate after Belgrade. Finally, they were prepared to exercise a moderating influence without giving up the legitimacy and substance of the issue of human rights. The Neutrals and the Nonaligned had considerable ground in common with many Western European countries.

In spite of minor differences on tactics and expressions of views in the Group on some specific issues, its members wound up their efforts around jointly sponsored proposals, regretting the lack of substantive contents in the Concluding Document of the Belgrade Meeting. It is more significant, though, that the Group assembled and coordinated its activities from the very beginning of the debates in Belgrade.

1. The Opening Statements in Belgrade

The CSCE had started from zero, moving all the time up towards a climactic and solemn finale in Helsinki (understandably with intervals of slow-downs and reversals). The Belgrade Meeting opened on a high note of faith and devotion to the Final Act, bogging down to an empty statement at the end. This peculiar progress of the Meeting affected in particular the positions and activities of the NN countries. The main engine responsible for this development was the controversy between East and West. The NN group had no hand in it. In fact, the Group tried to stop the downward movement. It made vigorous efforts to prevent the elimination from the Concluding Document even of agreed or agreeable texts. They consistently worked for the preservation of the momentum which they had injected into the proceedings during the opening stage and in the period of the presentation of proposals. As the Meeting proceeded, its changing mood affected also the goals and expectations of the NN group. This applies equally to their own initiatives and their reactions to the East-West polemics. In the beginning they displayed great activity and initiative, trying to turn the proceedings in the direction of process-dynamism and innovation.

As hosts, the Yugoslavs had the privilege of opening the Meeting with a message from the President of Yugoslavia, stressing the need to "examine under every aspect, in a frank fair way, what has been achieved so far and contribute, by patient work and by measures still to be defined, to make implementation of the Final Act more dynamic and more complete". The statement was a balanced and outspoken presentation of the position of the NN groups, based on the position of Helsinki, expressing the wish to avoid stalling but also pushing forward. Minić, the Yugoslav Foreign Secretary, picked up the thread:

> We are now faced with the obligation to consolidate the first modest steps we have taken in that sense and to complement them with new, more substantial and comprehensive measures aimed at strengthening security and mutual confidence.

The reference was to security in general and to confidence building measures in particular.

The statements by heads of delegations were begun in a similar tenor by the representative of Switzerland, Weitnauer. He also advocated this dynamism:

> . . . the last two years have shown us the considerable possibilities it gives us to give added impulse to European relations. These possibilities have been insufficiently exploited so far. Here we see one of the major tasks of the Belgrade Meeting. Together with our study of the past, it is for us to take initiatives which will make it possible to carry out that vast project of cooperation conceived in Geneva and Helsinki.

Weitnauer warned the Conference that failure to carry the CSCE process further would destroy, "the great expectations engendered by the signing of the Final Act of Helsinki."

As most other NN representatives Leifland, speaking for Sweden, promised tangible proposals on issues which might help to carry forward the process and help implementing the Agreements arrived at in Helsinki. Speaking of the possibilities to "improve cooperation and security", he said: "It implies rather that, within the framework of the CSCE and with the help of recurrent follow-up meetings, it will be possible to combine respect for the differences in our social and economic systems with an ever increasing exchange of views across our national frontiers." The Final Act of Helsinki was balanced and had to be preserved. But, he insisted that "at the same time, it is clear that the Helsinki Act is not just a document without a life of its own." It had proved to be a "challenging document" and acquired "new dimensions and created new expectations."

The longterm goals of the NN countries were also brought out in this series of presentations. In the outspoken and concise version of the Swedish delegation it could not be taken for granted that the present pattern of European security will remain unchanged in the long range. We do not want to exclude that one day it will be possible to dismantle the pact system on which our security is based today. This goal may, of course, seem very remote, but it would be absurd and dangerous to get used to regarding it as unattainable.

It is noteworthy that these goals were also, in the opening stage, fully shared by the Romanians. In their opening statement they underlined more or less the same basic views and expressed the same expectations as the NN countries.

As for human rights, NN countries had no doubt about the right to discuss the issue at the Belgrade Meeting. They did not accept the argument that any discussion of the protection of human rights in a country implied interference into internal affairs. In this respect they did not hesitate to express their views, or to confirm them silently, in spite of the fact that this position clashed openly with arguments of the Soviet Union. In fact, the rigid Soviet attitude was in striking contrast to the normal Soviet position when human rights issues in other countries are discussed in the United Nations.

The NN countries, however, insistently pointed out that the criticism should be moderated in view of its possible overall effects. They favoured a constructive debate, believing that it should serve the enhancement of human rights without jeopardizing good relations among states.

The importance of this issue and of the debate on it, was explicitly recognized by the Yugoslavian Foreign Minister:

We also believe that the realization of human rights should be constantly promoted through all-round, equal cooperation. Yugoslavia feels that the question of realization of human rights should be approached in a comprehensive manner and considered with a full measure of responsibility and realism, all this with a view to ensuring the constant implementation and further improvement of the provisions of the Final Act in this field.

The head of the Yugoslav delegation in the debate went on along these lines, concluding however, that "national sovereignty should not be invoked in an attempt to justify their violation."

This view was reiterated by Sweden: "The Swedish Government will not refrain from drawing attention to violations of human rights. We cannot possibly regard this as interference in the affairs of other nations. The Final Act gives us ground for holding this view. But governments must also carefully consider what best benefits the cause it wants to promote. This is a difficult but not impossible balance to strike."

2. The Proposals

The proposals submitted by the NN countries expressed more explicitly their goals and expectations for the Belgrade Meeting. The members of the Group were the first to submit proposals covering the whole field.

The Western delegations and the countries of the Warsaw Pact followed suit, and the flow of new proposals began to gain in momentum. Later, beginning with December, a new series of proposals emerged. The second batch of proposals was more interesting. It contained the considered views and proposals representing the final positions of the delegations. The first December draft of the NN group was a short document. It was apparently planned to be a possible basis for consensus; the group had by that time already redirected its activities to saving the Meeting from disruption. This is born out by the informal circulation of a fuller draft, issued on February 1, 1978. In the meantime East and West came forward with drafts which were much more detailed than the first NN December draft. The Group might have felt that it was proper to record a full statement of goals and expectations.

The second draft can then serve as the basis for analyzing the NN position at this stage. It begins by repeating the ten principles of the Final Act. The rest of the five thousand word proposal contains a large number of separate items, statements of intent, or clusters of measures together with proposals for specialized meetings. The sum of these detailed proposals can hardly be taken as expressing the position or the goals of the group, but is more likely to reflect two circumstances which influenced its members. The first circumstance is the necessity to keep within the limits of the Final Act, and the second is the fear of dissipating and of losing the momentum of the CSCE process.

From their point of view, the debate could attain positive results only if it served the advancement of the détente. After Helsinki, their aim was to widen the area of agreement among participants, and to deepen the trust. Embittered polemics were, therefore, seen as nefarious and a destructive threat to the still fragile structures built in Helsinki. Therefore, nothing remained but presenting a great number of modest proposals on all issues, hoping that the impact of number would compensate for the modesty. It could be said that the performance of the NN countries demonstrated their will to pull the discussion out of polemics, but not the proper instruments for doing so effectively. This explains also why the detailed proposals for the Concluding Document were made as late as February 1978, more than six weeks after the December proposal. Their expectations had by that time sunk very low in comparison with the initial optimism.

In the beginning of the Belgrade Meeting, the NN countries hoped that controversy about human rights would be a passing phase and not prevent a substantive agreement. In defending their basic goal, the NN countries tried to limit the polemics and inject dynamism and forward-looking ideas, based on the loftiest principles of the Helsinki Final Act. In the middle of the proceedings they were increasingly alarmed by the bitterness of the dispute. They tried to divert the discussion into calmer channels and made their proposals accordingly. This shift in tactics did not derive from a shift in the basic goals. It only reflected a shift in actual expectations and an adaptation of tactics to the situation. In fact, they were encouraged by the shift of the other delegations from restraint to a proliferation of proposals. However, very soon they realized that this abundance of proposals might well drown the last hopes for an agreed outcome in the form of a substantive Concluding Document. Gradually, it would appear that the character of its substance became less important than the filling of the void by a document with any substance.

It is, therefore, not of interest to analyze individual proposals submitted in the final stages of the Belgrade Meeting with the aim of ascertaining the intentions of the proponents. The battle became bogged down in the minimum requirement of the NN group to have even a token expression of dynamism. They were, of course, aware of the fact that no delegation, and certainly not the two major powers, would risk a complete breakdown. Even the shortest Concluding Document would hence reiterate the main ideas of the Final Act.

Regarded from the point of view of the NN countries, there was still a real danger of freezing the process of Helsinki. The Final Act might well share the fate of the Charter of the United Nations – untouchable but also a document the most important passages of which would be subject to controversial interpretations. The United Nations Charter is nevertheless capable of some slow and inadequate adaptation to the evolution of world affairs. This is due to the very general character of the Charter. The Final Act of Helsinki, however, is not a normative act or organizational framework, but the expression of a living process of the political situation in an important area of the world.

For the NN countries it was essential to develop and maintain the dynamism which had led to the convening of the Conference in Helsinki in 1973. The Group, therefore, fought for a substantive document, now more as a symbol of dynamism than a real movement forward. They accepted a meagre and empty document, because of two main features it still contained: the reaffirmation of the Helsinki Agreement (combined with references to the Belgrade Meeting), and the definitive and precise formulation of the continuation of the follow-up process, including the convening of a Meeting in Madrid. A further asset was the squeezing in of a Maltese formula on a meeting on the Mediterranean and two sentences on the détente, inserted on the insistence of Yugoslavia.

3. Drawing the Balance-sheet and looking ahead

No delegation, with the possible exception of the East European group, was quite satisfied with the outcome of the Belgrade Meeting. The NN countries were probably the most disappointed among the participants. Whatever the dissatisfaction of the West about the lack of affirmation of some points and principles, or the displeasure of the East (because of the reproaches), the Concluding Document gave them some satisfaction at least. The West had its criticism stand on record undiluted and unchallenged in the

Concluding Document; the East had the consolation that the criticism on human rights was not reflected in the statement at the end of the Meeting.

Only the NN countries had no consolation for the lack of dynamism, and for the stalling of the process of the CSCE. Not even diluted and modest proposals, which appeared to be noncontroversial per se, could find their way into the Concluding Document. They were eliminated because of the insistence of one side on the inclusion of the human rights issue, and of the other on leaving it out. The only possible agreement between the two major powers was an empty statement. This was best summarized by the Austrian delegate, Lidermann. "The Concluding Document before us, unfortunately gives us no detailed information of what has happened during our Meeting." He added that "the thirty-five participating states of the CSCE, after long and difficult discussions were thinking of their highest common denominator, whereas, at least in our Concluding Document, we have concerned ourselves only with the lowest." Arvidson, speaking for Sweden, regarded the set of proposals regarding confidence-building measures as the most regrettable case of omission from the Concluding Document and referred to all other proposals of which "hardly a trace remains" in the Concluding Document. But he insisted that "they still exist in our minds" and he expected this to give new impulses in the future.

The emphasis on confidence-building measures is not incidental. Among the proposals of the NN group, this issue was always standing high. It is closely connected with the logic of the basic goals of the Group. One way of injecting dynamism into the CSCE process could have been the expansion and the deepening of the détente in the normal civilian dimensions. The other could be the connection of the CSCE with military negotiations. In fact, the NN countries, acting at the time more individually than as a group, insisted from the beginning in Helsinki on the discussion of problems standing in between the MBFR and CSCE areas. There were even expressions of views that the two should be closely linked operations. In the face of immobilism in all other fields and the poor prospects for developing further any issue, the NN countries quite naturally revived their interest in the area of disarmament and arms control which was left only partly covered in Helsinki. Any progress in this field would have compensated amply for the lack of dynamism in other fields. The persistent efforts of the NN countries in the final stage of Belgrade to revive the proposals on confidence-building measures, and to expand them, expressed their determination that at least some movement forward was registered in the Concluding Document. But this was of no avail and to their disappointment no reference whatsoever was made to CBMs in the Concluding Document.

The quoted passage from the Swedish statement referred also to the future. This reference shows the growing agreement among the NN countries during the Meeting on laying the foundation for future cooperation, and in particular the follow-up process. Goals and expectations will obviously change in the future again. It is therefore difficult to speak of the goals and expectations of the NN group as once-and-for-ever-defined positions. The success of Helsinki greatly encouraged the NN countries, and created optimism. Expectations ran high and the goals were set high also.

During the last days of the Belgrade Meeting, we can observe the lowest ebb in the expectations of the NN countries. They stopped thinking of the Belgrade Meeting as a step forward. They were now interested only in saving it as a possible bridge from the sombre present to the hopefully brighter future. It was essential to secure the undisturbed flow of the follow-up process, to secure a meeting in Madrid. It should also be born in mind that the NN countries did not regard the deterioration of the situation in Europe after Helsinki as a consequence of any failure or shortcoming of the CSCE. To the contrary, the negative development was interpreted as something happening in spite of the positive outcome of the CSCE, which was seen also as a useful instrument for the development of détente in Europe.

The hopes expressed for the future, and in particular for the next meeting in Madrid, reflect this continued belief in the CSCE process and the determination to work in it and for it as a group and by individual efforts of each one of the NN countries. The basic goals remain unchanged, the expectations are rising with the approach of a new round. They may be based also on the hope that the polemic and rigid postures of the last two years may have served some purpose. The two major powers may have learned the limits of détente, as they had learned the limits of the Cold War in past years. After all, détente could not have been all smooth sailing without ripples, and occasional gales. In fact, the developments after Belgrade can easily be interpreted as the opening of an era of new, constructive approaches and dialogues between Moscow and Washington. If these contacts could bring about some improvement in the atmosphere, the conditions of the next meeting may be more like the climate surrounding Helsinki than the cloudy political weather of Belgrade.

Part II

PERSPECTIVES AHEAD: THE ROAD FROM BELGRADE

Chapter 6

LESSONS OF THE PAST, GUIDELINES FOR THE FUTURE

by *Karl E. Birnbaum*

The main significance of the CSCE process derives from the fact that it is a unique international effort in the collective management of both conflict and cooperation. This effort has taken place within a multilateral framework characterized by the formal equality of participating actors. It has addressed a multitude of problems in a region where on the one hand diametrically opposed political and ideological systems confront each other, but where on the other hand the benefits of cooperation have recently become increasingly tangible. At the time of the Belgrade meeting, the viability of that difficult and complex process was jeopardized by set-backs and dangers stemming partly from factors *external* to the CSCE framework itself, notably the unfavourable overall context of East-West relations and of super power relations in particular. But ever since the lengthy negotiations in Geneva 1973–75 that led to the compromise of the Final Act, the CSCE process has also been exposed to dangers *inherent* in that process. These dangers are related to two sets of developments emphasized by the CSCE negotiations: (1) The potentially destabilizing effect on existing political structures and power constellations in Europe; and (2) the tendency to produce bureaucratic ossification and self-incapsulation among those numerous officials engaged in this multifaceted diplomatic effort. The former development has mobilized potent forces in East and West with vested interests in the preservation of the status quo both in terms of international political configurations and domestic structures. The latter has at times generated an alienation between negotiators and their principals; more dangerously it has threatened to erode public support for the whole CSCE exercise.

These dangers notwithstanding, the CSCE framework, in the opinion of the present writer, continues to represent a novel and promising approach to the adequate management of intersystemic relations, in as far as it implies an effort to deal with the many problems that present themselves in these relations *peacefully* and to the mutual advantage of at least the *governments* of the thirty-five participating states. While this approach by no means guarantees the fulfilment of legitimate demands and aspirations of the *people* involved, it has inspired individuals and groups to articulate such aspirations and to pursue them both nationally and internationally.

It has been generally recognized that one of the most important innovations introduced by the CSCE into the politics of East-West relations was the fact that human and interpersonal issues, ranging from collectively formulated principles of human rights and fundamental freedoms to practical improvements in interpersonal contact and communication, were for the first time explicitly recognized as factors affecting inter-state relations.[1] It is equally obvious that this was primarily, although not exclusively, a Western preoccupation and that the significant concessions relating to this realm which the Soviet Union made in the eleventh hour of the Geneva negotiations have been largely "self-inflicted". To paraphrase a dictum of an experienced American negotiator, Gerard Smith, the Soviet leadership in 1975 clearly "lusted for the summit".[2] Faced with the risk of the summit meeting not taking place in 1975, Moscow preferred to consent to formulations in the texts of all three main sections of the Final Act – but particularly in Basket 3 – that went far beyond the expectations of many Western diplomats and observers.

What has not been sufficiently recognized by analysts of the CSCE is the fact that this novel dimension of East-West relations has *two* aspects, one, more general and abstract, reflected mainly in Principle 7 of the Final Act on respect for human rights and fundamental freedoms, the other more concrete and tangible, referred to particularly in the practical provisions of Baskets 2 and 3, the aim of which has been to facilitate interpersonal and inter-systemic contact and communication. Both aspects of the human dimension of the Final Act have been of immediate relevance for living persons, for human beings of flesh and blood. But by and large each of them has been aimed at different categories of people: on the one hand private citizens and particularly members of human rights movements in the East, whose actual enjoyment of human rights and fundamental freedoms *within their own countries* has on the whole remained curtailed; on the other hand, experts, scientists, artists and again private citizens who wish to meet, exchange information or simply see each other *across the East-West divide.*

In the period between the Helsinki summit and the Belgrade follow-up meeting, the more general and abstract aspect of the human dimension in East-West relations was given far greater prominence than previously. This in turn was due to several interrelated developments among which the most important were the emergence of monitoring groups of the Final Act in the East, the greater assertiveness of human rights movements in the Soviet Union and Eastern Europe in general and the forceful advocacy of human rights on the part of the incoming Carter administration. As a result of these developments, the distinction between the two aspects of the human dimension in East-West relations was blurred in terms of the operational goals of those states who have attempted to achieve some progress in this field. This became quite visible at the Belgrade meeting, efforts to the contrary of certain delegations, including notably that of the FRG, notwithstanding.[3]

The above observation leads us to the question of the extent to which the concrete and practical aspects of Baskets 2 and 3 have in fact been victimized by the new prominence of the abstract advocacy of human rights and by the fuzziness regarding the two aspects of the human dimension in East-West relations. If, as the present writer believes, this question must be answered in the affirmative, we face a number of follow-on questions such as: Did the performance of individual states in the CSCE context account for the victimization of the practical provisions in Basket 2 and 3? Or, are the causes of that development to be found *outside* the CSCE framework proper? And finally what conclusions if any can be drawn from the experience for the next follow-up meeting in Madrid? These important questions have been discussed in several contributions to this book. Another set of fundamental problems which events at Belgrade and subsequent developments epitomized and which the present volume deals with, relate to the *continuity of the CSCE process* itself. As indicated above, the viability of the CSCE framework would seem to be a common interest of all smaller European countries whether they belong to alliances or not. It is of particular importance to those states that do not take part in the Vienna negotiations on troop reductions in Central Europe, for whom the CSCE constitutes the only international forum – apart from the UN – where they can voice their opinion on European security issues. The document produced by the negotiators in Belgrade was a disappointment to all those who had hoped that this first follow-up meeting might add some momentum to the CSCE process. Many had expected that it would do so by deepening the implementation of the Helsinki document and also by doing what in fact the meeting was instructed to do in the Final Act itself, namely "to define the appropriate modalities for the holding of other meetings which could include further similar meetings and the possibility of a new Conference".

Neither of the two things was accomplished in Belgrade. The concluding document from that meeting did not contain recommendations or agreements on new measures that could further the implementation of the Final Act, although there is always the possibility that some of the proposals that were tabled in Belgrade will in fact be implemented unilaterally or in bilateral agreements. While there has been much talk about the procedures in Belgrade constituting a "model" for future meetings, no formal decisions were taken that spell out the modalities for such future meetings. The protagonists of the CSCE process have hailed the fact that agreement was reached in Belgrade to convene the next follow-up meeting in Madrid 1980. Some have portrayed this agreement as a guarantee for the continuity of the CSCE process. The decisions to meet in Madrid and to convene expert groups during the intermediate period give some reassurance, although obviously no absolute guarantee, with regard to the continuity of the CSCE process up to 1980. But the question that should be of concern to those who wish the process to continue relates to the prospects *beyond* 1980.

Major reversals with regard to the main parameters of East-West relations cannot be excluded. It would be particularly rash to do so in view of impending succession problems of the leadership groups in both Moscow and Washington. But even if the deterioration in super power relations could in some measure be insulated, the continuity of the CSCE process beyond 1980 seems far from safeguarded. The Final Act, to be sure, has been endorsed and confirmed and the document explicitly envisages several follow-up meetings, but it is difficult to visualize a continuous, viable CSCE process without progress in the implementation of the Final Act that is far more tangible and concrete than the results achieved to date. It should be obvious to all concerned that the results of Madrid must be qualitatively different from those of the Belgrade meeting if the CSCE process is to evolve. The crucial question facing the governments of the thirty-five participating states therefore is the following: What are the requirements and prospects for achieving levels of implementation that ordinary citizens of these states will be inclined to register as progress?

The experience at Belgrade and subsequent events suggest a number of "essentials" that will have to be heeded in order to maximize the prospects for an outcome at Madrid that will satisfy popular expectations. Two would seem to be of particular importance. Firstly, that historically, the CSCE has not been the main engine of East-West détente but rather its product. Consequently, the ups and downs of CSCE negotiations have reflected the state of East-West relations at a given moment. Yet one of the unique features of the CSCE lies in the fact that due to the delicate balance in the formulations in the Final Act it is the only framework of East-West negotiations where the inherent interdependence between international stability and the human dimension of inter-systemic relations has been explicitly and authoritatively recognized. But while the Final Act reflects and registers this fundamental interconnection, the provisions of the Helsinki document do not automatically guarantee deference to what would seem to be the imperatives of interdependence between security and human rights. The extent to which the appreciation of this interdependence will grow, is crucially affected by the performance of the main actors at CSCE negotiations. Hence the need for a balanced approach to the review sessions envisaged in the follow-up clauses of the Final Act, a point strongly and convincingly argued in the contribution of Jerzy Nowak. The challenge before the West in this connection seems to be to convince the Eastern powers that Western advocacy of human rights is not only motivated by concern for the predicament of individuals, but also by the conviction that deference to the aspirations of human rights movements is the best guarantee that tensions generated by unfulfilled aspirations will not lead to upheavals that may jeopardize international security.

Secondly, another "essential" is to appreciate a basic difficulty inherent in the follow-up process of the CSCE. According to the Final Act, that process includes essentially two stages: (*a*) the review of implementation and (*b*) the elaboration of new proposals, aimed at enlarging the scope and extent of future implementation. As the experience at the first follow-up meeting has shown, it is psychologically difficult to pass on from the first to the second stage. The review exercise necessarily involves a considerable measure of mutual criticism on the part of participating states and is thus not particularly conducive to creating the atmosphere of understanding that is required for a venture in constructive co-operation which can produce new proposals and give a fresh impetus to the CSCE process as a whole. It seems important that in preparing for Madrid, the function and contents of new proposals to be tabled at the forthcoming meeting are carefully reassessed. Under no circumstances should the practice at Belgrade of presenting proposals purely for the purpose of satisfying the mass media or of neutralizing unacceptable suggestions of the other side be repeated. If the CSCE process and indeed East-West détente is to have a future, the governments of participating states will have to make a more determined effort to distinguish between common, complementary and compatible interests. The greater the emphasis in their policies is on common and complementary elements the easier it will be to make the difficult step from reviewing past performance to charting the road to a better future.

Notes

1. *First Semi-annual Report by the President to the Commission on Security and Cooperation in Europe. Report submitted to the Committee on International Relations*, 94th Congress, 2nd Session, Washington, Dec., 1976, p. 10.

2. Cf. Gerard C. Smith, "Negotiating at SALT", *Survival* XX:3, May/June, 1977.

3. Cf. Per Fischer, "Das Ergebnis von Belgrad. Das KSZE-Treffen in seiner Bedeutung für den Entspannungsprozess." *Europa-Archiv* 8/1978.

Chapter 7

THE CSCE FOLLOW-UP PROCESS: AN ASSESSMENT

by *Luigi Valsalice*

After the unsatisfactory results of the Belgrade meeting and in view of the forthcoming Madrid meeting of 1980, it is quite legitimate to enquire into the validity today of the follow-up clauses of the CSCE Final Act signed in August 1975. This query is even more valid if we think that we are witnessing a transformation in the significance of détente as a long-term process in the East-West dialogue in Europe and in the world as a whole.

It would seem difficult to deny the fact that the real importance of the CSCE has to be gauged by the efficacy of the implementation of the follow-up clauses and of the follow-up process after Helsinki. The question is whether the CSCE process still means something in the fabric of a lively East-West debate in Europe; or whether the CSCE has been a diplomatic experiment, which had its roots in a different period of intra-European relations, and is no longer relevant in the present situation.

Let us recall that at the beginning the CSCE was intended, in the view of the East Europeans, as a scheme to achieve recognition of the status quo in Europe (recognition of the GDR and of the inviolability of frontiers) and at the same time as the starting point for the creation of a security system founded on some kind of permanent organ. The East European countries thought it obvious that a pan-European conference, after having established the rules of the game in Europe in accordance with a conservative and static view of future developments, would decide to establish a system in order to implement these rules and to guarantee the immobility of the system in its entirety.[1] But – and it is a big but – such a system was not to be conceived ever as a tribunal charged to pass judgements on how these rules had been respected by the members of this European club; the system could only be permitted to act as a clearing house for bilateral and multilateral consultations. Here we are confronted with a major point.

In the East, the détente was conceived as an irreversible process, an achievement of the East-West dialogue from 1955 onwards and of the CSCE in particular. The détente was thus viewed as something to be strengthened, if necessary, but no longer to be conquered through daily action and continuous efforts of the European states. The aim of détente was peace and cooperation, and each state had a clear-cut right to assess by himself whether an act of another state was to be considered as an infringement of the rules of détente. The bilateral consultations were there to stay, as a cornerstone of the security system, for only through such regular consultations could the interests of the socialist community be safeguarded and a development avoided which would imply recourse to evaluations by a body that, due to its very nature, might, sooner or later, exercise supranational functions.

The whole debate on the follow-up before and after Helsinki was centered on this point. Let us go deeper into it. Before 1972, the Western countries, with the very active EEC countries in the front line, declared themselves against all projects for a security system as an offspring of the CSCE, which they had accepted only after considerable hesitation. This unwillingness to accept as a working hypothesis the offer coming from the East was mainly due to two considerations:[2] firstly, the fear that in view of the retrenchment of the United States, the influence of the Soviet Union within a European security system would be dominant; and secondly, the conviction that the emergence of a pan-European system should *follow* but never precede the process of political unification within the framework of the EEC.

Actually a third element should be taken into consideration. The possible results of a pan-European conference were unknown factors until 1973 – that is until the first phase of the CSCE in Helsinki. No responsible person in the West was inclined to entertain the idea of a "system" whose scope and functions would be dependent on the results of such an uncertain enterprise.

How did these three central considerations impinge upon CSCE negotiations in the period 1972–74?

The complete transformation of the CSCE project, which in the course of these negotiations changed beyond recognition, made it less likely that the Soviet Union could assume the role of the pre-eminent force in a pan-European context. In fact, the Soviet Union and her allies found themselves in a difficult position, as they were confronted with the common firm will of the Western countries to provide the CSCE process with a dynamic perspective, opening up prospects for a different quality in the relations between peoples and individuals. This was not only reflected in Basket 3 subjects but also in relation to the issue of the territorial status quo; for the normalization of relations with the GDR and the Berlin settlement had become *prerequisites* for the convening of the CSCE, and consequently the debate on the inviolability of the borders took on a new aspect: it established the legality of a change of borders by peaceful means and with mutual consent, thus negating the Soviet thesis that the territorial and political status quo in Europe could under no circumstances be altered without Moscow's assent.[3]

The second consideration proved to be very stimulating. It could hardly be said that in those crucial years 1972–74 the EEC made sweeping progress towards political unification, but the confidence was there. Some joint positions during the crisis in the Middle East in 1973, the Copenhagen declaration on the European identity, the development of relations with the United States, the positive result of the British referendum and above all an ever deeper political concertation for and within the CSCE[4] could rightly be considered as convincing evidence that the EEC was there to stay as a political community. Furthermore, after the vague recognition by Mr. Brezhnev in March 1970 of the European Community as a "reality", the tolerated presence of the EEC delegates at the negotiating table in Geneva implied a further step in the direction of EEC recognition by the Eastern powers. Thus, the CSCE exerted a positive influence in enhancing the awareness of the EEC members that they were part of a thriving political community.

The third factor ended up with being one of the most important at the negotiation level. Western scepticism at the early stage of the CSCE process in November 1972, much sooner than could be foreseen by the optimists, gave way to a sincere feeling of self-confidence. Much credit for this development is due to the NN countries. But it is also quite clear that the far-sighted vision of the Nine and of NATO countries perceiving the CSCE as a unique opportunity to put forward the ideals of the Western and pluralistic society, was a decisive factor. The link between the results of the CSCE and a mechanism for its follow-up very soon became a cornerstone of the Western position. That was the main reason for the Western refusal to discuss – more than vaguely – the follow-up process during the preparatory meeting in Helsinki 1972–73; for their adament opposition against the setting up of any working group in Geneva on the follow-up before the concrete results of the CSCE negotiations could be assessed; and finally, for their proposals of an intermediate period of evaluation after the closing of the CSCE.

This idea – mainly French – of an intermediate or probation period after the final conclusion of the CSCE, is very important not only as a key to the interpretation of the relevant clauses of the Final Act. It is important also because it meant a different approach to the future evolution of détente as a continuous process. It should be recalled at this point that in 1973–74 considerable pessimism prevailed with regard to the usefulness of the CSCE. Disillusionment about the whole exercise was reflected in the lack of interest shown by mass media and even by political leaders. The CSCE appeared to be no more than a vanity fair, full of words and with no concrete results forthcoming.

Therefore, it appeared politically mandatory to think of a system that could provide for a gradual but tangible implementation of the provisions of the Final Act through successive stages with political thresholds to be verified one by one before proceeding to the next stage. Thus, after the CSCE, the technique of a step-by-step approach, which had been the Western way of thinking and acting since the preparation for the CSCE started,[5] was to continue as the only effective method for ascertaining that the CSCE was politically worthwhile. Besides, the probation period also provided an opportunity to express in a straightforward way the scepticism prevailing in the West with regard to the willingness of Eastern powers to carry out the substance of the Final Act.

Such an attitude was justified in view of the very contents of the Final Act. The rules which it proclaims – and this applies not only to Basket 3 – portray a society which is after all more akin to Western than Eastern conceptions. Would it have been necessary to repeat rules which are commonplace in Western societies, if the purpose had not been to try to induce the East to conform to them? The balance between the three baskets has been a miracle in equilibrium and in diplomatic verbiage. To ensure implementation in the spirit of that equilibrium, it had to be placed in the perspective of the basic idea that the Western societies were assumed to be the model for the relations between the governing authorities and the citizens. Everybody is free to believe in his brand of democracy, but it is the Western brand which pervades the Helsinki document. It is not by chance that the Eastern dissidents refer to the Final Act, when they try to change the Soviet fulfilment of socialist democracy.

The probation period, as initially proposed, was based on the following considerations: to evaluate how the CSCE resolutions had been implemented and to assess at the same time the conditions for better relations among the member states in the future; to table proposals, aimed at promoting the goals of the CSCE at deepening the provisions of the Final Act; to provide for several meetings of experts on specific subjects and/or for meetings of high officials, which might eventually lead up to a second general conference.

The West was not opposed to the idea – promoted particularly by some neutrals – of experts' meetings on several subjects to give more substance to the actual carrying out of the contents of the Final Act. But in connection with the efforts of the NN countries in 1974 to achieve a closer coordination of these technical bodies, the Nine in particular were anxious to draw a sharp line between the obligation to comply with the provisions of the Final Act on the one hand and the continuation of the multilateral process on the other hand, with the latter opening up prospects for a second general conference. The reason was self-evident: a second conference would be the outcome of a new political evaluation, based on a careful consideration of all factors affecting East-West relations within and outside Europe. It was essential to avoid pre-empting that evaluation by premature decisions in the ongoing CSCE negotiations. This Western policy was clearly in sharp contradiction with the Soviet line. After a last statement on the subject of April 19, 1974, the Soviet Union and its allies suddenly became very silent with regard to the CSCE follow-up. The Soviet Union to be sure insisted on the possibility of future new conferences, but it appeared to be a tactical move only: new conferences on what, where, and for which purpose? Much to the dismay of its allies, particularly Poland – not to mention the lonely stand of Romania – the future after Helsinki seemed to be something to which Moscow was now inclined to pay lip service only.

Thus, the reluctance of the Soviet Union, the caution of the Nine, the indecisions of most of the NN countries that did not want to run the risk of jeopardizing the outcome of the CSCE, these were the factors that produced a specious unanimity on the decision to include in the Final Act follow-up clauses that were in line with most of the proposals of the Nine.

Détente, whatever it is, must evolve in accordance with the real possibilities of international life. It could be jeopardized or superseded by events, for détente is after all not an inherently permanent condition. New relations may emerge and new concepts could be introduced signalling the obsolescence of a process which developed after the cold war, but which has remained frail and open-ended.[6] This changing mood was symbolized by the Belgrade meeting in 1977.

Was Belgrade a failure? Was it rather a half-success? The answer can be twofold. Those who thought it possible to produce drastic changes in many facets of the relations among the European states and within some of those states were disappointed. Those on the other hand who were seeking a continuation of the dialogue on the basis of the Final Act with all its ambiguities, but also with its wisdom, were moderately satisfied.

Before the Belgrade meeting the Soviet Union tried to launch new initiatives, notably some pan-European conferences on specific subjects (energy, transportation, environment). But those attempts ended in total failure. They were makeshift proposals to forestall what to Moscow must have appeared as the danger of the too concrete results of the Belgrade meeting or, in more general terms, too wide-ranging interpretations of the follow-up clauses. The Soviet approach to these great intra-European projects could have been a first step along the road leading to significant changes in the exact meaning of these follow-up clauses. According to the Soviet scheme, the Belgrade meeting and the follow-up process in general were supposed to serve only a perfunctory function: to recognize the existence of a favourable international atmosphere and thus to sustain détente by verbal pronouncements rather than deeds. The essential link between the follow-up clauses and the gradual implementation of all the provisions of the three baskets of the Helsinki document would have been completely lost.

Belgrade was a modest meeting epitomized in a very eloquent way by a Final communiqué without substance. Should we infer from it that something was wrong in the wording of the Final Act?

The contrary would seem to be the case. The probation period after Helsinki was thought of as a way to clarify whether the provisions agreed upon were viable enough to form the basis for the normal life of the European states. The best method to test that point was to verify the degree of implementation provided for by national laws and regulations, or by current practices. However, beyond this bureaucratic verification, the clauses on the probation period also allowed to wait patiently for an assessment before entering into a new round of pan-European negotiation of any sort.

The very polemics at Belgrade on human rights, the excessive amount of Western proposals on the most different subjects and the Soviet proposal on military détente are all developments that attest to the viability of the Final Act. They have dispelled any doubt that the words contained in the Final Act had acquired sufficient vitality to prove that its provisions were able to produce a debate on essential problems, even though it did not bring forth operative conclusions.[7]

After Belgrade the CSCE process has continued with expert meetings: Bonn, Montreux and Valletta.

The Expert Meeting on the Scientific Forum held in Bonn in

June–July 1978 was on the whole quite successful. It may seem difficult to imagine how a lively debate with diverging views could unfold on the role of scientific research in East-West relations. Yet, when the organization of research and the contacts that it entails were related to human needs, the worries of the East to see the human rights issue emerge became immediately visible. The final document, approved after extenuating and sometimes surrealistic discussions, was not considered as very satisfactory by the Western scientific world. The opening up of scientific and cultural cooperation between East and West is all the time hampered by the fundamental disagreements on the modalities for a freer flow of ideas and information.

It is quite clear that according to Eastern conceptions even scientific activities in the realm of medicine or mathematics have to be reconciled with ambiguous political formulas, such as the strengthening of peace and détente. Thus, an intellectual activity, whatever its practical purpose, must never ignore the fundamental tenets, Marxist-Leninist doctrines and the ultimate goal of building a new society.

At Montreux (October–December 1978) basic disagreements were voiced as a direct consequence of some of the debates in 1972–75. If the neutrals were in favour of a system to ensure the peaceful settlement of disputes with general and compulsory application, the West was in favour of taking into account some compulsory factors to enrich already existing methods of settlement. The Eastern states wished to avoid creating anything that might involve compulsory measures, claiming that existing differences between the two social and economic systems and the present practices of the States must prevent such a system from functioning; at most, they could accept compulsory consultations. The purpose of this strategy was quite clear: nothing should be set up in terms of supranational bodies or binding rules that could weaken the freedom of choice and decision of any State. The states were to retain their sovereign prerogatives unimpaired. It is almost superfluous to recall that the Swiss proposal for a peaceful settlement of disputes, as introduced initially in Helsinki, was aiming exactly in the contrary direction. The Soviet refusal to accept more binding follow-up clauses during the Geneva negotiations was also motivated by the wish to avoid a detailed examination of the far-reaching original Swiss proposal.[8]

The assessment of the Valletta meeting on the Mediterranean (February–March 1979) is more difficult. With regard to the participation of the Mediterranean states it was not a success. These states had shown considerable interest in the CSCE at Helsinki and at Geneva without participating in the negotiations themselves – not being considered as "European" in the strict sense of the word. At Valletta, however, with the exception of Egypt and Israel, none of them turned up at all. Syria limited herself to asking for the presence of the PLO – a request conflicting with the CSCE rules – and disappeared. Algeria, Lebanon, Morocco and Tunisia absented themselves from the meeting altogether.

It is quite obvious that nobody ever thought that the Mediterranean could become a full-fledged subject for a European conference – and its follow-up – particularly if military and political issues were to be included, as insisted upon by Malta. The main aim of several CSCE countries was to stress the principle that a serious discussion of European security could not take place without considering the Mediterranean as an element of that security: Europe after all is not a landlocked region and the Mediterranean has always been an integral part of Europe.

The lack of interest shown by the Arab countries in the follow-up of the CSCE may have had many reasons. First of all the Arab countries have their own problems of paramount importance, intensified in the more recent past by the Egyptian-Israeli peace treaty: the CSCE is not immediately related to these major preoccupations. Taking into account the seriousness of those central problems, the Arab states do not seem to think that a CSCE meeting on marginal technical subjects could tackle the most important questions in the area, which concern them directly. Finally, the CSCE philosophy itself, based on the ideas of an East-West détente, does not conform to their own political conceptions, bearing on the subjects which are vital to them.

Whatever the reasons for the Arab attitude, it is quite clear that the political goal of the follow-up clauses on the Mediterranean was not reached at Malta: the association of the non-participating Mediterranean states did not materialize. Perhaps this objective overtaxes the capabilities of the CSCE for the simple reason that it is focused on a region which is not central to the CSCE process itself. Yet, the states participating in that process cannot ignore the Mediterranean dimension in the future without losing an important aspect of European security.

Viewed from a different perspective, the Valletta meeting could be considered as the only meaningful follow-up of the Final Act. The more than twenty recommendations on economic, scientific and cultural subjects – including some political issues such as the recommendation on migrant workers – represent a very business-like implementation of the letter and spirit of the Final Act. What is strange about this proliferation of recommendations is that the thirty-five CSCE states agreed on deepening some parts of Baskets 2 and 3 in connection with the Mediterranean, even though the rest of the Mediterranean countries were absent. They did so yielding rather passively to the activism of the delegations from France and Italy. The danger resulting from this development could have been a regionalisation of the follow-up process, contradicting the very philosophy of the CSCE. That danger was averted, inasmuch as the contents of the recommendations applied to all the CSCE states without exception. On the other hand, these states have not been prevented by the CSCE to pursue co-operation among themselves in the Mediterranean, e.g. in the context of the EEC or the North-South dialogue.

One more aspect of the Valletta meeting has been the substantial support which the Soviet Union and her allies gave to the Franco-Italian and other Western proposals and, in fact, to the West as a whole. Possibly the Eastern states were anxious to prevent the meeting in Malta from pursuing an "extremist" path towards the setting up of some permanent committee for the Mediterranean, and thought it was better to agree with the West without presenting proposals of their own. In the absence of the traditional East-West confrontation, the NN countries were unable to act as a mediating group, and the presence of Malta among them certainly did not facilitate such a role which in the past, in Helsinki and Geneva, had been very fruitful.

Let us sum up our findings and try to assess the role of the follow-up clauses of the Final Act in view of the forthcoming Madrid meeting. The Final Act was a miracle in ambiguity and balance, but on major points rather a success for the Western notion of the CSCE process. The follow-up clauses were thought of as an instrument to gauge very cautiously the results of a diplomatic enterprise, the scope of which was very vast indeed. The review of the probation period was substantially a failure at Belgrade and a moderate success at two out of the three meetings convened afterwards on specific subjects. Those meetings widened the verification process started at Belgrade and carried it further on a technical level without the political acrimony that poisoned the atmosphere at Belgrade. What next then?

The continued follow-up of the CSCE should not be limited to a sterile debate on what is right or wrong in the fulfilment of the Final Act's provisions.

It is easier to express criticism after a failure than to reconcile such failure with a program for future action. In effect, the West tried at Belgrade to impose its own interpretation of the follow-up clauses. It has rightly been underlined that the follow-up clauses were meant to test the political will to continue the détente process and to materialize it by a gradual implementation of all the provisions of the Final Act. However, did these follow-up clauses justify the tabling of a host of new proposals, relating particularly to those sections of the Helsinki document – Basket 3 – where the formulation of almost every substantial provision was the result of a delicate compromise between conflicting *Weltanschauungen*? It is true that the strategy of the West at Belgrade – reflected also in President Carter's attitude – was a logical development of the original Western conception of détente as a dynamic process promoting a different quality in East-West relations. But the necessary propitious conditions for the realization of that conception, which would have involved a major effort to persuade the East to give up its traditional static view of détente, were not present in the East-West context prevailing in 1977.

Thus, the Belgrade failure – or half-success – was not caused by some inconsistency in the follow-up clauses, but rather by an unbalanced use of its provisions.

This is not to suggest that the Western countries should radically change their course of action at the next follow-up meeting in Madrid. Adaptations and adjustments of attitudes will certainly be required but no reversal of fundamental positions. For it would be an incorrect interpretation of the CSCE follow-up clauses to accept the Eastern view that the review meetings are to be limited to the gaudy recognition of the persistence of détente, and to cling to the principle of "mutually acceptable conditions" to the point of reducing everything to the level of the most conservative position among the thirty-five states. The political dimension of the CSCE process must be preserved at Madrid as well; it is an intrinsic element of the follow-up clauses of the Final Act.

The point to be discussed is thus whether this political content of the follow-up clauses should be expressed by proposals aimed at gradually modifying the overall context of East-West relations in Europe; or if it should be presented in a more provocative way in order to establish the fact that after Helsinki all European states must conform to the model of Western societies enshrined in the Final Act.

This basic dilemma could also be expressed in different terms. Should the follow-up provisions be interpreted as pushing the CSCE states (and above all the Western states) towards a vigorous reaffirmation of the fundamental dynamic objectives of the CSCE process or should everybody content himself with a step-by-step approach hoping to get some minor, useful, realistic results? It is not a trivial dilemma, since Madrid will after all be the second trial of the validity of the follow-up clauses of the Final Act, and could well become the last. In the latter case it would also be the end of the CSCE process.

The question appears even more important in a field which is mainly political, although in Geneva and Helsinki it was considered as technical: the military measures. In Belgrade, the Soviet Union tabled ambitious and ambiguous proposals on the so-called military détente. The Budapest meeting of the Warsaw Pact in May 1979 came out with analogous suggestions, but in this case outside the framework of the CSCE follow-up clauses, not unlike the French proposals on conventional disarmament in Europe.

It is not our task here to discuss the possible strategy of the different groups in Madrid, but one point is essential. We have seen why the CSCE follow-up was formulated as it was in the relevant clauses of the Final Act: the East had not obtained all it wanted and therefore was willing to reduce drastically the impact of the follow-up and the West was distrustful and tried to avoid entangling itself too much in the follow-up process. The compromise was possible because in the bargaining the Soviet Union had committed itself to come out from Helsinki-Geneva with a solemn ceremony, as it eventually took place with the signature of the Final Act at the summit meeting in Helsinki 1975.

The West should, then, inquire into the possible Soviet motivations in Madrid 1980. An extension of economic cooperation to overcome the difficulties of the Comecon community? The military détente or a project for a non-aggression treaty as a way to reassure the West? A consolidation of good relations with Western Europe to isolate the Chinese? It could be argued that the Eastern states should try to ascertain Western preoccupations: in that case they should be reminded that the issue of human rights will remain high on the agenda of Western governments.

For both sides, the follow-up clauses are there to be used to continue the CSCE process. If among the thirty-five states a consensus can assert itself, viewing that process as a useful one, with a potential to enrich the European dialogue beyond the scope of traditional détente concepts, then the Final Act and its follow-up provisions will have proved to be viable political instruments.

Notes

1. Cf. Hassner, *Change and security in Europe*, Adelphi Papers, no. 45 and 49, London, February and July 1968.
2. Cf. Ferraris (*a cura di*), *Testimonianze di un negoziato*, Padova 1977, *passim*.
3. See Valsalice, *Affari Esteri*, 1975, no. 28, October 1975, p. 695.
4. Cf. Höhn, *Aussenpolitik der EG-Staaten*, München 1978.
5. See Ferraris, op. cit., pp. 47 and 88.
6. Cf. Valsalice, *Trent'anni di alleanza atlantica*, Roma 1979, p. 123.
7. Cf. Delbrück-Ropers-Zellentin (eds.), *Grünbuch zu den Folgewirkungen der KSZE*, Cologne 1977, *passim*; see also Birnbaum in: Andrén & Birnbaum (eds.), *Beyond détente*, Leyden 1976, p. 139–157.
8. See Ferraris, op. cit., p. 308–320.

Chapter 8

EXPECTATIONS AND DISILLUSIONMENT

by *Nils Andrén*

It goes without saying that any evaluation of contemporary political and diplomatic events – like the Belgrade Meeting and the whole CSCE process – must suffer from many limitations. Time perspective, emotional and political preferences, institutional and national engagement, all contribute to making current analytical efforts provisional and preliminary. Given the limitations of the possibilities available for this kind of research and analysis, the method of mixing knowledgeable scholars with diplomatic practitioners has great advantages. It brings the "source material" within immediate reach of the analysts but it is by no means a riskless undertaking. The CSCE process still remains an ongoing operation and it would hardly be realistic to expect the participants and practitioners to strip themselves of all the garments of a political or diplomatic actor.

In writing these concluding observations, the author is hence very much aware both of the advantages in important respects of not being an insider, of not being politically or personally involved, but also of the handicap of being an outsider to the CSCE process. The hope is that the lack of sensitivity to the atmospherics and details of the process may at least in some respects be compensated by the distant observer's interest in overall perspectives.

For a realistic evaluation of the CSCE process and of the causes for expectations and disillusionment, it is important to know the need felt by the actors concerned for this particular element in the détente pattern. The basic question is simply: who needs the CSCE and for what purposes?

Security and cooperation in Europe is the professed purpose of the CSCE process. The political goal of the CSCE may be described as the optimal realization of removing distrust and exploiting all possibilities for expanding a genuine community of interest and general mutual understanding. The idea of being able to fulfill these high ambitions, however unrealistic, is a necessary political utopia. The process itself is less ambitious. It is more related to present difficulties than to future fulfilment: tangible success is very desirable but the most important thing is to continue the process, as evidenced by a great number of participants in the CSCE movement. The consolation is that the relative failure of Belgrade will be followed by Madrid. And the hopes focused on this new phase are sufficient to claim Belgrade as the success in the process, even if no goals were achieved. Both as a goal and as a process, European security – like détente in general, of which the CSCE is not the cause but an outflow, as Karl Birnbaum has rightly reminded us – has many facets, created by a variety of hopes and ambitions, of forces and interests.

The main actors in the CSCE process are all represented in this book. They have been selected among the thirty-five states involved on the assumption that there are five major groups of actors whose attitudes are likely to decide the future of the CSCE process: the two superpowers, their clusters of European clients and the NN group. It is abundantly clear – as evidenced already, over and over again in the previous chapters – that these five groups conceive the purpose and possibilities of security and cooperation in different ways. Summarizing expectations, disillusions and prospects for the future, their views may serve as both a starting point and as indicators of possible directions.

As long as the European security pattern remains bipolar in its fundamental character and is dominated by the superpowers around whom the majority of European states are grouped as more or less enthusiastic clients, the process of détente in Europe is closely tied to the benefits, both regional and global, that the superpowers expect to derive from it. This observation surely also applies to the CSCE game. Indirectly, Richard Davy emphasizes this aspect in his reminder that the Western side had little bargaining power left at the Belgrade Meeting and that this fact constituted a fundamental difference in comparison with the negotiations in Helsinki and Geneva. Curt Gasteyger underlines that dominating superpower attitudes, Soviet damage limitation against Western "massive retaliation" and "assured graduated criticism", left little room for bargaining.

The Soviet Union had attained its primary goals already with the adoption of the Helsinki Final Act – essentially a definitive recognition by the West of the post-World War II political borders in Europe. The *cordon sanitaire* – mainly of WP-aligned states – was explicitly accepted. Any faint hope among the Soviet clients, however unjustified, for support from the West for a change became if possible bleaker than before. However, the price to be paid by the Soviet bloc for this recognition was heavy. Principle 7 and Basket 3 included undertakings which even in a Marxist reading could hardly be understood as compatible with the Soviet political system. Hence both were regarded by the West as important gains, constituting, together with the review mechanisms, a dynamic element in the process, as already emphasized by Luigi Valsalice. Unless the Soviet Union sets new goals for her CSCE activities, the realization of which requires Western concessions or other active participation, the West is unlikely to have any significant bargaining power derived from what is conceived as the long range ambitions of the Soviet Union. If these overall ambitions – as defined by Alting von Geusau – are to promote the victory of socialism (in the Soviet meaning), then, of course, little is to be gained for the "non-socialist" West by conceding Soviet demands. The question remains, as to whether more limited, short-range goals may provide a new dynamo for bargaining between the superpowers in the CSCE context. Thus far, there is no certain answer.

In Helsinki, as it has been observed, the United States remained, on the whole, passive. Its goal, if any, may well have been limited to keeping their European allies happy by its presence and to maintain a profile which could help to reduce the lingering impact of colonialism and corruption. In Belgrade the situation was different. Vietnam and Watergate belonged to the past. The "realists" had finally disappeared with the fall of the Republican administration; with the advent of President Carter, the "moralists" held the reins of office. The new Administration found, perhaps to its own surprise, that the Final Act offered a tool to enhance political credibility at home by broadcasting human rights abroad. Richard Davy has underlined the difficulties of reconciling this policy with NATO alliance cohesion and bilateral negotiations with the Soviet Union. However, intentionally or not, the American attitude also fits into another political pattern during recent years – the cooling of détente in order to add spirits and muscles to the Western alliance. This development has led some Western politicians and observers to question détente as a present reality or to abolish the very term in their political vocabulary.

What all this amounts to, is that the superpowers are very uncertain supporters of the CSCE process. For global détente, as far as they strive for it, they have their own, bilateral instruments. So far, they have mainly been interested in using the CSCE as a lever for domestic or global bloc interests; to promote an ongoing regional European process appears to be important only as a means, not as an end in itself. For the future it is hence in all probability left to the Europeans themselves to protect and expand the regional usefulness of the CSCE as a process. European détente concerns in the final analysis the survival of a Europe which for the superpowers is not only the two clusters of allied clients but also, in a strategic sense, primarily an area of bloc-to-bloc confrontation and in a military sense, judging by the deployment of forces, the chief battleground in any future war between them.

Nuclear or not, any major war in Europe is unacceptable to the European states. This underlines the vital interest of the peoples – especially in central Europe, on both sides of the great divide – in combining the necessary power-balance with an effective détente. What is true of the bloc-aligned borderline states in Europe is also true about the NN states, whose chances in a European war of commanding respect for their neutrality is by no means assured. For the NN states, however, success for European détente, relaxation of tensions between the blocs, is equally important in peace, creating a general political climate in which they can pursue their own political and economic interests without raising suspicions on either side. Hence, it is quite logical that the NN group has emerged as the most consistent and constructive supporter of the CSCE process.

The Nine of the European Community – eight of whom are also

members of NATO – had, as explained by Alting von Geusau, been able to enhance their own identity in Helsinki, obviously due to the low American profile. In Belgrade they found only limited scope for doing so. To a great extent they were merged in the wider NATO identity. Hence the expectation that for the short-term future "détente will no longer be a valid subject for presenting a European identity." It is probably very important to underline short-term. If – and it is a big if – the CSCE process survives this short term, which is likely but by no means to be taken for granted, it is not improbable that interests in regional cooperation will assume new significance within the CSCE framework. With a lower profile on human rights it might be possible to realize cooperative undertakings, e.g. in commercial, industrial and environmental fields. Policies of this kind underline the importance of interdependence but could probably be effected without the CSCE structure. The same is very likely true about confidence-building measures (CBMs) which could easily and perhaps more effectively be accommodated in an expanded M(B)FR context.

The overall impression of the Nine is that they had few strong expectations but also that they were prepared to present and promote a number of proposals outside the disputed territory of the Seventh Principle and Basket 3. However their "babies" were lost in the general quarrel over human rights. On this issue the Nine could claim to have been, in principle, as outspoken as the United States, but not as obstinate. They were tempered by their strictly European interest in maintaining favourable conditions for developing East-West cooperative relations. As long as the superpowers regard SALT as their major forum for matters of East-West détente, it is as important for the Nine as for any other group of European states to preserve the fora for international negotiations between the superpowers to which they have access.

The place of the East European states in the détente/CSCE pattern is more difficult to evaluate. These states have to exist under political and economic regimes and conditions representing a necessity which is imposed from the outside and not an outflow of an undisturbed domestic political process. The contribution by Jerzy Nowak deals specifically only with Poland. However it underlines the importance of a general European dialogue as an opening which can penetrate the rigid bloc structure. But it also emphasizes the importance of a "realistic cooperation", meaning among other things cooperation within the framework of the restrictions set by the character of the Communist system and by the fears of penetration by free access for "subversive" ideas or persons. The problem is clearly formulated in Jerzy Nowak's observation that "there has been no experience of peaceful cooperation lasting long enough to provide a basis for confidence in its usefulness and trust that it does not imply dangers for internal stability and for the social order." It is not surprising that the East European reaction reflected deep disappointment with the confrontation spirit evolving at the Belgrade Meeting. However, it is also clear that the reaction, as reported in this volume, is characterized by a strong plea for patience: "It cannot be forgotten that the Belgrade Meeting was only a stage in the process of implementing the CSCE Final Act; it was only a fragment of the multilateral process initiated in Helsinki."

The review provided by Leo Mates of the NN countries, their actions and reactions, underscores the argument that the CSCE process is a European interest. The NN countries, operating in the CSCE context both as independent actors and mediators anxious to assure constructive results of the negotiations, entered the review conference with considerable ambitions to preserve "the momentum of change". The existence of a European interest, distinctly separate from the bloc-pattern of suspicion and confrontation, is clearly brought out by the reference to NN-West European similarity of views during the preparatory stage preceding the Belgrade Meeting.

When all ambition for constructive compromises to keep the dynamics moving had to be sacrificed in order to achieve an empty document on which everybody could agree, the disappointment was probably greater in the NN group than among any other participants. Two quotations from the Finnish closing statement seem to summarize not only the NN countries' reactions but also those of several other European countries, on both sides of the great divide. The first is simply: ". . . my government had higher expectations with regard to the result of this meeting than what has now been achieved." And the second, as a parting shot: "Tempered by the experience gained here we thus look to the future with guarded optimism."

Both the necessity of détente and the fascination of the negotiation game seem to create an indomitable optimism about tomorrow among those involved in the process. In spite of the disappointments of today, Leo Mates – both an actor and an analyst in the CSCE context – is not dejected by ripples and gales during the sailing. "The expectations are rising with the approach of a new round." He is also looking hopefully to the development after Belgrade as the opening of an era of new, constructive dialogues between Moscow and Washington. However, the development of the CSCE process proper seems hardly to justify expectations for a major change in this process. The documents on the expert meetings after Belgrade, referred to by Luigi Valsalice and reprinted in Part 4 of this book are certainly proof of a continuing dialogue but hardly reassurance of future progress. Like all other European groups the NN countries have to find their chief consolation and hope for the future in the fact that the Belgrade Meeting could agree on a new review conference in Madrid. One reason for the lack of success in Belgrade was – according to the previous analyses – the fact that only two years had lapsed between the Helsinki Conference and the Belgrade Meeting. Exactly the same, too short period of time has been decided upon between the Belgrade and Madrid meetings.

It has been amply demonstrated that the CSCE process has the potential of providing a new lever for the West to irritate – if not to penetrate – the Eastern system of domestic repression. The reactions in the form of domestic protective measures against dissidents propagating the ideas laid down in the Final Act – both before and after Belgrade – are clear indications of Soviet and Communist awareness and watchfulness in relation to the new dangers. For the non-socialist participants in the CSCE process it is an important question if and how the human rights weapon can be used again. The incompatibility of the ideas prevailing in the two ideological blocs makes the human rights issue into a weapon so devastating that it could well wreck not only the CSCE process but also many other gains during the era of détente. It is clear that there is a strong awareness of the restrictions imposed on the use of this weapon also in the West – including the United States – and on the inescapable conflict, at least in any discernible time perspective, of human liberty in the Eastern block with regional stability and hence also with détente in Europe. In a sense it is an insoluble dilemma. For the West the opening of the closed Communist systems appears as a necessary condition for mutual trust and confidence. In the East such a development would undermine self-confidence and indeed break up the whole political system.

The prospects for the future, according to a unison evaluation by both experts and practitioners in the CSCE process depend very much on the balance between the two possible "uses" of the CSCE: the one to promote bloc interests in order to change the European power balance by penetrating the adversary system, the other to continue the search for areas, small or big, in which cooperation and contact can be preserved and expanded without creating suspicion and conflict. The first alternative, it has been argued here, is particularly tempting for the superpowers. The problem is obviously that it may easily be self-defeating. In order to survive a policy of change must be conducted in such a manner that it may be claimed with some credibility to be a genuinely cooperative effort, not a political offensive. However, if the balance between cooperation and offensive is maintained, the likely result may well be that the progress of the process is stalemated although the process itself may survive, at least in an institutional sense as a diplomatic undertaking. The "minimalistic" optimists, represented also in this volume, may remain at least moderately happy.

The conclusion is that the future of the CSCE process is mainly in the hands of the superpowers. If they play the power game they will either wreck or – as in Belgrade – paralyze it. If the superpowers decide to maintain a lower profile, the future of the process depends on what the Europeans are able to make of it. If the CSCE process cannot survive the strain imposed by rival ambitions in exploiting its potential uses, this does not necessarily mean that what it stands for is lost. For if it is true – as Curt Gasteyger confidently concludes – that "the Soviet Union will soon discover that she, too, is becoming a prisoner of interdependence" this means that economic exchange and communications will increase. A gradual development of this kind seems to be the only possibility for increasing interdependence, community of interest and confidence between the two blocs without a dangerously destabilizing effort to change either system or both. If this is true and if at the same time the power game inside the CSCE process remains too tempting to be resisted by the two supergrands, then it might well be in the best interest of European security that the CSCE process is permitted to fade away.

This observation is not a forecast. A more probable future for the CSCE process is that it will continue and thrive on continuous assurances of unflinching support by the majority of participants. Its life expectation may well be enhanced by the interest of the players in continuing a game where clear gains or losses are impossible and where success simply means to avoid breaking up the game.

Part III

DOCUMENTS

OPENING STATEMENT

by *Mr. Goldberg*

MR. GOLDBERG (United States of America) (After reading certain remarks in Serbo-Croatian):
Ladies and Gentlemen, for the benefit of the Yugoslav interpreters who may find my Serbian not intelligible, and for the benefit of the delegates who do not possess my comprehensive knowledge of Serbian, I shall translate that into English: Mr. President, distinguished Excellencies and other colleagues, first of all I wish to thank President Tito as well as the members of the Yugoslav Government for the outstanding organization of this conference. We are more than grateful for the facilities and support they have so generously provided for the conduct of our work. It is particularly symbolic that this Conference is held in a nation which has done so much for so long to promote security and cooperation in Europe.

Fellow delegates, I shall ask to say a personal word. It is a great privilege of mine to make my address under the Presidency of Ambassador Sherer. There is no American who has done more and more competently to promote the purpose of CSCE from the long arduous journey from Helsinki, to Geneva, to Helsinki, to Belgrade in the Preparatory Conference, until now; and I should like all of you to know the high regard I personally and our Government hold for him.

Two years and two months ago the leaders of our thirty-five nations assembled in Helsinki to conclude – with their approval – the Final Act of the Conference on Security and Cooperation in Europe.

This week we are beginning in Belgrade a new phase of the process they initiated. We are embarking, as many speakers have said, on a mutual examination of our experiences in implementing the Final Act. We are also seeking together new means of solidifying and building from the foundations laid in Helsinki.

Our task is part of a great and ancient enterprise: the search for security, the advancement of cooperation in Europe. This Conference is one more step toward that high goal, one part of the broader process of reducing risks of confrontation in Europe and of replacing them with opportunities for cooperation.

This meeting is both an expression and a result of considerable improvements in East-West relations. In turn, what we accomplish here in the coming months can have a direct impact on the further development of détente.

I have been designated by President Carter to speak here as the representative of Cyrus Vance, the United States Secretary of State. I carry with me the President's and the Secretary's deep, personal commitment to advance the goals of the Final Act and the work of which it is such an important element. Both the President and the Secretary are dedicated to working constructively with all nations represented here, regardless of ideology, to help fulfil the Final Act's commitment to improved European security and cooperation; and this is a subject in which the United States has a vital and concerned interest. For Europe is the continent from which we draw our origins, Europe is the continent to which we sent our young men twice in the struggle to protect Europe, its viability and its independence.

Two corollary principles make the Helsinki approach unique. One is our rule of consensus, the recognition that every nation represented here, small or large, should take part on an equal footing in decisions which affect the future of Europe. The second is also crucial: the tie, formalized by the Final Act, between the freedom and welfare of each of our nations, and the freedom and welfare of each of our individual citizens: the two are inseparable. Let me reaffirm in the most positive terms the wholehearted commitment of the United States to the pursuit of détente. Let me also state our considered view that a deepening of détente, a healing of the divisions in Europe, a relaxation of tensions in Europe, cannot be divorced from progress in humanitarian matters and human rights. The pursuit of human rights does not put détente in jeopardy. Rather, it can strengthen détente, and provide a firmer basis for both security and cooperation.

The United States wants, the United States seeks to build upon and enlarge the scope of East-West understanding. For my Government is convinced that this Conference in Belgrade must not be the end of the CSCE process. Rather, it must be an occasion to inject fresh momentum, new insights, into that process. The true test of the work we do together lies not only in the conclusions we reach – and we are mandated by the Final Act to reach conclusions. It lies also in the higher goals we set and in the energy with which we set about meeting them.

My Government, my delegation, will do its best to provide new impetus to our process both here in Belgrade and in our overall policies towards Europe and the world:

– We will conduct the review of implementation on the basis of the unity of all sections of the Final Act and the equal value of all the principles. And that is what the Final Act says.

– We will make clear our intention to honour the political commitments in this document and to utilize fully the practical opportunities which it opens.

– We will discuss concrete problems in detail in the appropriate forum of the conference, problems of both past and future implementation.

– We will conduct our policies in Europe fully aware of the fact that CSCE can only bear part of the burden for guarding the peace. There must also be progress in other efforts at détente; and the benefits of our efforts must be applied throughout Europe and throughout the world. Berlin, for example, remains, and will continue to remain, a basic testing place of détente. This divided city must continue, as the Final Act says, to receive the benefits of the Final Act. Berlin must prosper under the Quadripartite Agreement, free from crisis, if détente and CSCE are to succeed.

President Carter made our country's commitment to a world détente north and south, east and west, explicitly clear in his address to the General Assembly on Tuesday last, just the other day.

Just as the United States goal for Europe is one of peace, so at this Conference we seek – and we join others who have said so – no confrontation. We have no desire at all to trade debating points. Instead, we want to exchange ideas between you the delegates and the countries that you represent on how better to implement the Final Act. We seek a thorough, non-political straight-forward, candid, frank and detailed review of implementation. And through that review, we seek to help formulate new measures which can give added concrete expression and momentum to the basic commitments of the Final Act.

The first obligation we all share is to conduct a candid review of the promises each of us has made, the promises we have kept, and the promises we have yet to fulfil.

The assessment my country has made of the overall record of participating states over the last twenty-six months shows encouraging evidence of progress. But the progress displayed is not progress enough. It still falls short of the goals of the Final Act, and perhaps just as important if not more so, of the high expectations among the people of Europe and the people of the world that the Final Act aroused. Those expectations remain and are valid expectations. We must all be frank in judging that many of them remain unmet.

If we are to have an accounting it is only right and just that I start with my own country. In general, the Act codified standards which reflect American policy in dealing with other nations and with our own citizens. Nevertheless, in response to the Final Act we have looked closely at our own behaviour and, where we have found the need and the means, have acted to improve our conduct. In particular, we have taken two steps recently regarding the Final Act pledge to "facilitate freer movement and contacts." First, President Carter this year removed all restrictions on travel abroad by American citizens. Second, with President Carter's support Congress recently relaxed our visa requirements, so that people wishing to visit the United States will not be excluded because of political affiliation or belief, except in the rarest instances, not really related to their politics.

Moreover, in the field of human rights, President Carter on Tuesday at the United Nations redeemed a pledge he gave last spring by signing the International Covenants on Human Rights. American adherence to these pacts has been a matter of personal concern to me, since I negotiated those pacts for our country, and, of course, to many others for a decade.

The President is pledged to pursue ratification of the Covenants through our constitutional process. Meanwhile, his action at the United Nations is an earnest indication of our good faith and a proof of the positive impact the Final Act is having in the United States.

In the spheres of commercial, cultural, educational and scientific exchanges, we have done much and have much yet to do. For example, the United States Government has made a special effort to inform our businessmen about provisions of the Final Act affecting their opportunities to enter and work in markets with which they have not always been sufficiently familiar. This year, we signed our first cultural, educational, and scientific cooperation agreements with Hungary and Bulgaria; and we concluded negotiations on a similar agreement with Czechoslovakia. With the Soviet Union, we renewed several scientific cooperation agreements.

Meanwhile, in some other signatory nations, we have seen a well-intentioned and productive effort to implement the principles and provisions of the Final Act. In the spirit of candidness I must say to you that in some nations in the East, advances have been only modest, and are still far below the Final Act's standards. And there are individual cases under the Final Act where forward motion has been stalled or even reversed.

Under the stimulus of the Final Act, some progress has been made in bettering relations among the participating states and this is all to the good. The exchange of goods, knowledge, people, and ideas has expanded in some measure. But substantial obstacles do remain to travel and the flow of information between one part of Europe and another, but as I have said these have already been diminished somewhat. This improvement can be seen simply in the numbers of people who have been able to leave their old homes for new ones in Europe, America, and Israel. These results mean real individual humanitarian, personal happiness, and we here must reaffirm our resolve in a humanitarian spirit to speed that result.

Likewise, in translating our shared political undertakings to the area of military security, the Final Act has brought about another exchange, very promising because it is in the military field, generally a field where secrecy is stressed, sometimes far too much. Confidence-building measures, including advance notification of manoeuvres and exchange of observers, have made openness a virtue in a field where as I have said secrecy was once instinctive and all too prevalent. It was with great personal pleasure that I saw a newspaper picture the other day of a military observer of the Soviet Union observing manoeuvres in Germany of NATO Forces. But we must go further. We have made only a very modest beginning in a very difficult area.

Thus we can see some progress: We can see it in terms of individuals and families reunited after being separated by war, by accident, by history. But we must recall, we cannot forget, we cannot mute our voices about those who remain apart.

We can see progress in business contacts that become business contracts helpful to all participants in a business dealing. But we cannot overlook the still inadequate supply of relevant economic data on which the growth of business confidence depends.

I have spoken to businessmen in our own country who have the greatest good will in this area to forward free trade throughout the world and they tell me that it would be extremely helpful and productive if all of the signatories were to make available essential economic data upon which important business decisions, freer trade, confidence can take place.

We can see progress in books translated, performers in the arts applauded, students instructed, art exhibits exchanged and scientific theories tested. In our own country we have had the benefit of some of the great paintings in the Hermitage, and our country was very interested in seeing what the vast treasury of that great museum holds, and we have had several benefits from other countries. But here too I must say the openness and ease of access to scientific exchange, to scholastic exchanges, has not been as great as really they ought to be. Thus we cannot be satisfied with the record of implementation. Although we take satisfaction with the progress that has been made, the standards we have set together should be higher if the goals of the Final Act are to be realized.

Let me illustrate some areas in which we in the United States feel old practices have not been changed sufficiently to meet the imperatives of the new Helsinki spirit, in somewhat greater detail than I have done so far.

In educational exchange programmes, it is not enough to increase the number of scholars involved; rather a prerequisite for such an increase is improved freedom for scholars and their research. All of us should open our archives to reputable scholars. There is no reason for not doing so, and scholarship can only take place, if it is to be productive, if archives of all of us are made freely available. What value is there, for example, in financing a student's work abroad, when for months he is denied admission to an essential library, or archive or newspapers and when, having finally been admitted one day, he is not permitted back the next – even to collect his notes?

Also in seeking "to facilitate the freer and wider dissemination of information of all kinds," we cannot point convincingly to progress while international broadcasts are subjected to continuing interference.

It is my strong personal belief that no country in Europe would have its security jeopardized and all countries in Europe would benefit if there were complete access to all radio programmes and television programmes; I think life would be more interesting for all of us if this indeed were so. Finally, while steps have been taken to ease travel and working conditions for journalists via multiple visas – by the way a great accomplishment of Belgrade, of Helsinki – those advantages are jeopardized when visas are made conditional on a correspondent's agreeing not to contact certain sources of information and opinion. This is a deep-felt view by our press, indeed some of our newspapermen have risked gaol rather than reveal their sources, and therefore to exact as a condition for granting a visa a stipulation not to contact certain sources runs contrary to a deep-felt view in my country.

Finally, while real progress has been made in reuniting divided families and concluding binational marriages, satisfaction with these developments must be balanced by regret that many long-standing cases – many may be too strong a word, as I remember the figure, they are not so many; they are relatively few – are not resolved. I say to myself when I think of that 'Why are they not resolved? What bigger hardship can there be in humanitarian, personal relations when a man and wife coming from different countries cannot be reunited so that they can live in happiness and raise their families?' It has seemed to us that the resolution of what ought to be routine cases is often arbitrary and capricious, and that new bureaucratic obstacles are imposed on people in this area and also in the area of divided families.

I think everybody in this hall will agree with me on the importance of family life as one of the great problems of modern civilization, particularly in what we call the developed countries – I always rather did not like that phrase, I did not know exactly what it meant – let us say Europe. What conceivable purpose is served by not allowing families to be reunited when we believe and emphasize today that one of our goals, and I think we shall succeed, is to improve the quality of family life? But in addition to this humanitarian goal, this runs contrary to the Helsinki promise gradually to simplify exit procedures. The results make it very hard for me to see the workings, and again I quote the Final Act, of a "positive and humanitarian spirit" when an ill and aged husband is denied, after long years of separation, the company of his nearly blind wife and their daughter.

Equally difficult to understand are restrictive provisions on the right of the individual to travel and emigrate. That right is established in Article 13 of the Universal Declaration of Human Rights, and I quote it: "Everyone has the right to leave any country, including his own, and return to his country." Now, the Universal Declaration of Human Rights is not unrelated to the Final Act; as we lawyers would say, it is incorporated by reference because all of us pledged in the Final Act to "act in conformity" with the Universal Declaration, and we have given specific emphasis to that promise in the Final Act's provisions on family reunification.

The two years, or more than two years, since the Helsinki summit are particularly short when we set them against the historic divisions we are trying, through the Final Act, to bridge. Some of the deepest differences, in all candour as we have heard, among the participating states lie in views on the status of the Individual in relation to the State. The issue of human rights represents the widest gap between the ideals and practices of East and West. It is a sensitive subject on the international agenda, but one which we believe, and which I propose can be and should be dealt with in an understanding manner recognizing this difference in ideology. It must be discussed in order to facilitate further progress on the Final Act.

Precisely because the distance between our views in this conception is so great, we must all work to narrow the divide, because, as has been said – and I repeat – people are involved, and they are involved in the Final Act. It is not a simple process, as I can bear personal witness. In my own country a mere 15 years ago many Americans were denied the right to vote, but through governmental commitment to an ideal and constant efforts to reach that ideal, this blemish on the American record was removed, and happily today we follow the principle of 'one person, one vote'.

Other serious blemishes remain and our efforts to remove them also remain constant. I am realistic, as you are; the process is inevitably a gradual one, but the efforts like ours are what make progress in human rights possible under the Final Act.

In the United States, and it took some time for us to come to this conviction, we also realize that human rights encompass economic and social rights as well as political and civil liberties. It is our view that one set of values cannot be stressed at the expense of another. Rather, it is the combination of these rights and the respect in which governments hold them all, which offer the best promise that all can be realized.

We have said that there has been emphasis on human rights, and you know, of course, President Carter's statements in this area, but I should like to say with due respect to my President that he makes no claim to have discovered human rights. He would agree with me that concern for these rights is not new, either to Americans or to the other states taking part in the Conference; it is enshrined in Article 1 of the Charter of the United Nations, also incorporated by reference in the Final Act. It is enshrined in the Universal Declaration of Human Rights, and the Final Act in Principle 7 binds all the participating states to recognize the universal significance of "human rights and fundamental freedoms, respect for which is an essential factor for the peace, justice and well-being necessary to ensure the development of friendly relations and cooperation among themselves as among other states."

American policy – evolving from a history of political development and repression with deep roots here in Europe, and nurtured by the efforts of other nations from which we drew – has long pursued that vision. It is explicit in our Bill of Rights. And in our days of poverty and distress and in war and in the aftermath of war, it was not possible to get our constitution adopted unless there was a commitment that there would be a Bill of Rights. It animated the Four Freedoms proclaimed by President Franklin Roosevelt, if you remember his famous statement: "All people everywhere are entitled to freedom from want, freedom from fear, freedom of speech and freedom of religion, for which Americans last fought on this continent in the war against fascism." It was also part of the heritage of President Kennedy when fourteen years ago he launched the fresh initiative for world peace; he asked, in the great address at American University, "Is not peace in the last analysis a matter of human rights?" and, anticipating Helsinki, he proposed an "agreement on a freer flow of information and people from East to West and West to East." And this has been bipartisan with us because when such an agreement was concluded in Helsinki as part of the Final Act, President Ford echoed his predecessors' words. He said: "The founders of my country did not merely say that all Americans should have these rights, but all men everywhere should have these rights."

I have said that President Carter did not find human rights, indeed he didn't, but I give him great credit for bringing human rights to the forefront of world opinion, and on many occasions this year President Carter has set forth his own commitment to the continuity of American policy in the area of human rights – whether political, economic, social, or cultural. At the United Nations last March, he stressed that the

> "search for peace also means the search for justice . . . and the search for peace and justice means also respect for human dignity. I know perhaps as well as anyone that our ideals in the area of human rights have not always been attained in the United States, but the American people have an abiding commitment to the full realization of those ideals. We are therefore determined to deal with our deficiencies quickly and openly."

And I have never believed that the people of the United States in this regard are different from the people of any other country in this globe.

Search for human dignity, the search to be treated as a person in one's own right and to be accorded the privilege of an individual – I regard to be an attribute shared by men and women and children all over the world.

It is in this spirit of our feeling that this concept is not an American concept but a concept you all share – that the United States and your people share – that the United States delegation will speak about human rights and basic freedoms here in Belgrade. And we have much to learn from that exchange of views.

Let me further illustrate some of our concerns. The Principle 7 guarantee of religion and belief means to us that expression of faith must not be penalized by loss or reduction of educational or career opportunities. People should be free to worship without fear or state interference in their choice of ministers, literature, and houses of prayer.

Similarly, and I am quoting the Final Act, the "freedom of thought and conscience" we have all pledged to respect must have breathing space to survive and to flourish. Its expression should not be censored. Its exponents should not be imprisoned or exiled for making their thoughts known.

Moreover, the "legitimate interests" of "national minorities" in all of our states require respect for unique cultural and linguistic heritages, and active policies to preserve these traditions and achievements for future generations.

My fear for my own country is that we will become too homogenized. I would hope that this great country of ours will preserve the pluralistic tradition of our country, preserving the cultural values we derive from Europe and now increasingly from Asia and from Africa. I would regard that to be a strong cement rather than a divisive factor in solidifying our country into a people, one people.

Our governments have assumed the responsibility, again quoting the Final Act, to "promote and encourage the effective exercise" of these rights. And in Principle 7 we subscribed to, and I quote, "the right of the individual to know and act upon his rights and duties" in the field of human rights. The response of citizens to that challenge, alone and in either private or public groupings in many signatory states, as has been mentioned most recently by Lord Roberts, has been heartening evidence of the Final Act's healthy impact on all of us. In my own country, we have benefited by the dedication, candour, and commitment of our Commission on Security and Cooperation in Europe, a unique executive, legislative commission set up by act of Congress signed by the President to monitor performance of the Helsinki Act. Its valuable work will be reflected in what we do here in Belgrade; and we are honoured by having its members as part of our delegation.

All the more, then, we are also obliged to register vigorous disapproval of repressive measures taken in any country against individuals and private groups whose activities relate solely to promoting the Final Act's goals and promises.

Any such repression is contrary not only to the spirit but to the specific words of the Act that we all agreed upon and signed at the highest level. At this meeting we should reaffirm and we should give support to the valuable role to be played by individuals and organizations, in their own countries and in international organizations to help make that pledge a reality.

Mr. President, in conclusion I should like to say this to the delegates:

In the coming weeks, the United States delegation will focus its efforts in a constructive manner on improving relations among the participating States. We are here to help strengthen prospects for cooperation, and to help move closer towards what should be the noblest common goal of the Conference: to give the process of détente a human measure and a humanitarian face.

I have been asked repeatedly since I arrived here: "Are you seeking a confrontation with the Soviet Union?" My answer has been a categorical "No". We are not seeking a confrontation. We are seeking cooperation in an Act signed by the Soviet Union and the United States and all of you at the highest level. And we are prepared to conduct a non-polemical dialogue in the appropriate working groups and otherwise, recognizing ideologies are different, and to arrive at measures that will carry out the Final Act, and I join in what has been said by some speakers: the Final Act needs no amendments, none at all. What it needs is implementation; better implementation than it has had.

In that spirit we will consider and, as appropriate, support new measures to improve implementation. We seek opportunities for improvement in the following areas which are explicit in the Final Act:

- promotion of human rights;
- further execution of confidence-building measures;
- qualitative expansion of scientific, economic and commercial data exchanges;
- easing of travel for journalists and businessmen;
- freer access to printed and broadcast information from other countries; and
- fuller opportunities for scholars and scholarship.

This is a very incomplete list, others have been mentioned and we do not exclude any proposal from our consideration. We can see there are opportunities to promote the exchange of literature, television programmes and culture of all kinds. We have the facilities to do so, technologically. Let us come to grips with that problem. There are possibilities for exploring, in such appropriate agencies as the UN Economic Commission for Europe, the co-ordination of approaches to such pervasive problems as environmental pollution, mentioned in a speech made by the distinguished delegate of the Soviet Union. And there is a great potential for expanding trade and for sharing the benefits of technology.

However, our success will be measured not merely by words on paper, even if we were to agree upon a paper at the end, but rather by what we all do both here and at home after this meeting ends. Together, if we are faithful to what was done at Helsinki, we must give the process of implementation direction, higher goals and fresh momentum, to ensure that when we next meet in a similar assembly – because the Final Act contemplates periodic meetings – we can record greater progress than we have made today.

In our work we will need patience, perseverance and perspective. This Conference in Belgrade is one stage of a dynamic process and a continuing dialogue. And we must always recognize that Helsinki is part of an even larger effort to build more secure and more humane relations among our nations and peoples, and in that effort, of course, the staggering weight of armament upon all countries of the world bears an important role. It has been discussed in other forms but we cannot escape the reality of what the world is confronted with.

We are nearer the beginning than the end. The Conference must give the people of the signatory countries and the people throughout the world a first report of its first progress. It would fail utterly the people, let alone governments, if it does not demonstrate to them our shared commitment to go further. We owe them our best efforts and results better than those so far achieved.

OPENING STATEMENT

by *Mr. Vorontsov*

MR. VORONTSOV (Union of Soviet Socialist Republics) (interpretation from Russian):
Mr. Chairman, first of all, the Soviet delegation would like to express deep gratitude to the Government and people of Yugoslavia for their great efforts in organizing this meeting. We are particularly thankful to the President of the Socialist Federal Republic of Yugoslavia, Comrade Josip Broz Tito, who has addressed a warm message to the participants in the Belgrade Meeting.

Mr. Chairman, a little over two years have elapsed since the Helsinki Summit adopted the CSCE Final Act – a short period of time considering that the Helsinki accords form a broad platform for action by states in their many-sided relationships for decades to come. Full implementation of all the principles and accords laid down in the Final Act as a programme for joint action by states is a long-term process and it is to give Europe a new image – to transform it into a continent of lasting peace, guaranteed security and fruitful cooperation.

But even this limited time since the Conference has confirmed how constructive its results are, how urgent is the need to give effect to them. Peace in Europe has become more stable, one can say more durable, and multiple links between nations have become considerably wider and richer. On the whole, détente is being consolidated and strengthened. This trend is prevailing in international relations, for today's world can offer no sound alternative to détente.

During the last two years many topical issues concerning life in Europe today have been examined by political leaders and statesmen, as well as at other levels, in the course of bilateral and multilateral talks; important political documents have been signed, numerous agreements have been concluded to promote economic, scientific and technological links as well as human contacts which make inter-state relations increasingly comprehensive and substantive. A more peaceful situation in Europe is also furthered by the application of the confidence-building measures envisaged in the Final Act, in particular by prior notifications of major military manoeuvres and the invitation of observers to attend many of them.

At the same time, during these two years it has become obvious – and this is an important point – that the pace of implementation of the provisions of the Final Act is dependent to a great extent on the general level of détente, on the state and on the development of bilateral relations among the participating states. Those who oppose détente – and such circles do exist in the West – by the same token hinder the implementation of the provisions of the Final Act.

What is meant by the concept of détente? Above all, it means overcoming the cold war, a transition to normal and stable relations among states. Détente means willingness to resolve differences and disputes by peaceful means through negotiation rather than by force, threats and sabre-rattling. Détente implies a certain degree of confidence and the mutual capacity to take into account the legitimate interests of other states. It is that very approach which is reflected in the joint Statement signed last summer by the leaders of the Soviet Union and France on the relaxation of international tension. We believe that this first major bilateral document of that kind can provide a useful stimulus and serve as a model in building good relations between all states. Seeking to expand détente and to extend it to other parts of the world, the Soviet Union, as is well known, has submitted for the consideration of the thirty-second session of the United Nations General Assembly a draft Declaration on the Deepening and Strengthening of Relaxation of International Tension.

The Soviet delegation would like to emphasize the importance of maintaining a favourable atmosphere in inter-state relations.

The elimination of the legacy and vestiges of the "psychological war" from the ideological struggle is a prerequisite for the improvement of the international atmosphere.

Noting the progress achieved so far in restructuring international relations on the principles of détente, peaceful coexistence and cooperation, we cannot but recall that immediately after the triumph of the Great October Socialist Revolution, V.I. Lenin, the founder of the Soviet State, in his first foreign policy document, universally known as the Decree of Peace, clearly stated our realistic approach toward the cardinal issue of our time – that of eliminating wars and ensuring a durable peace which is in the interests of all the peoples of this planet.

The viability of the ideas proclaimed by the Decree of Peace has been borne out by history itself, including the success of the all-European Conference and the process of implementation of the principles and accords adopted there. The declaration of Principles laid down in the Final Act constitutes the very code of peaceful coexistence, the main elements of which were set forth in Lenin's programme for democratic peace.

The Soviet Union has been working steadily for sixty years to translate those principles into life. They were further developed in the Programme of Further Struggle for Peace and Cooperation and for the Freedom and Independence of Peoples adopted by the Twenty-fifth Congress of the Communist Party of the Soviet Union. They are in accord with the peaceful aspirations of all countries and peoples and represent a realistic basis for ensuring a lasting democratic peace and international security in Europe as well as throughout the world.

Recently the Soviet Union has undertaken yet another unprecedented initiative. The new Soviet Constitution that is being adopted after many months of nation-wide discussion – in which over 140 million people took part – contains a clear-cut description of the foreign-policy objectives of the Soviet State: ensuring peace, consolidating the security of peoples, securing general and complete disarmament and broad international cooperation. Thus the new Constitution reflects all the ten principles of mutual relations among states proclaimed in Helsinki. Now these major provisions of the Helsinki accords are embodied in our Constitution. I would like to express the hope that other States too will find it possible to incorporate in legislation – in the forms appropriate to the rules and customs of each country – the agreed principles of inter-state relations.

The Soviet Constitution makes a general and formal statement of the principle of equality and the right of peoples to chart their own destiny, which for many years has been a reality of life in our country of many nations. The new Fundamental Law defines even more fully than before the socio-economic and cultural rights affecting the basis of everyday life. The political rights and freedoms of USSR citizens have been further developed.

The General Secretary of the CPSU Central Committee and President of the Presidium of the USSR Supreme Soviet, L.I. Brezhnev, said in his address to the Special Seventh Session of the USSR Supreme Soviet on October 4th that "the new Constitution is indeed a condensed result of the entire 60 years' development of the Soviet State".

In our country human rights and fundamental freedoms are more than just proclaimed and laid down in laws, they are guaranteed by our socio-economic system itself.

It is a fact that unemployment is non-existent in the Soviet Union. Soviet citizens enjoy free medical care. Free education at all levels has brought our people to the heights of culture, stimulated millions to cultivate their talents and made possible scientific and technical achievements of world renown. The socialist system ensures wider rights and freedoms, continuing betterment of living standards as programmes of socio-economic and cultural development are carried out and international peace is strengthened.

Mr. Chairman, since Helsinki the Soviet Union has consistently intensified its efforts to strengthen the meaning and enhance the effectiveness of the principles that the participating states undertook to be guided by in their mutual relations and that make up the political core of the Final Act. These principles should become a permanent factor in the political reality of Europe and should be consolidated in bilateral relations in various fields. They have already been embodied in a number of important bilateral political documents signed recently by the Soviet Union with other countries, including such West European countries as France, Italy, the Federal Republic of Germany, Finland, Portugal, Sweden and Belgium. Political contacts and consultations, including meetings at the highest level, have become broader and richer. This promotes greater confidence and better understanding between states. It is imperative to work to further enhance the effectiveness of these principles, above all through their strict observance by each state and through their incorporation into bilateral and multilateral cooperation.

Mr. Chairman, the Helsinki Final Act is permeated throughout with concern for peace in Europe, for greater security for all the European peoples. All the participating states should, in line with their obligations under the Final Act, make efforts to reduce the military confrontation on the continent and take practical steps in the field of disarmament. This would complement political détente by military détente. This is the intention of the well-known proposal, put forward after the all-European conference by the Warsaw Treaty countries in the 1976 Bucharest Declaration of the Political Consultative Committee, for a treaty to be concluded by all the CSCE countries on the non-first use of nuclear weapons.

We are convinced that such a Treaty would make an important contribution to the removal of the threat of nuclear war and hence war in general and to the strengthening of mutual confidence, for if nuclear weapons are not used by any State first, there will be no second, third, fourth or fifth State to use them. Besides, talks on that subject and their successful outcome would open up new opportunities for progress in the talks on troops and arms reduction in Central Europe.

The question of preventing nuclear war is viewed by the Soviet Union as a matter of primary importance, which is stressed by the fact that our government has submitted a special draft resolution on that subject at the current session of the United Nations General Assembly.

The Soviet Union, together with other socialist countries, has more than once emphasized that a thorough normalization of international relations requires putting an end to the division of the world into opposing military blocs. For many years they have been expressing their readiness to dissolve the Warsaw Treaty Organization simultaneously with the North Atlantic Treaty Organization and – as a first step – to disband their military organizations. Last November the Political Consultative Committee of the Warsaw Treaty countries again appealed to all states to refrain from actions which could lead to an extension of existing closed groupings and military and political alliances or to the creation of new ones. This proposal still stands.

Over recent years we have made a total of over seventy proposals aimed at ensuring peace and disarmament and making détente really operative.

The close interrelation between security and cooperation is reflected in the very title of the all-European Conference. Indeed progress towards political détente provides new opportunities for equal and mutually beneficial cooperation between states, while that cooperation in turn consolidates and deepens détente, makes it meaningful and improves the political climate. Prompted by these considerations, the Soviet Union has come up with the well known proposals to further all-European cooperation in the field of the environment, development of transport and energy.

Problems arising in these three spheres have certain common features. Firstly, these problems are assuming a special and increasing urgency for all the peoples of the densely populated industrial regions of Europe and North America. Secondly, due to the nature of these problems, many of them can, in the words of the Final Act, "be solved effectively only through close international cooperation". And finally, all-European cooperation in those fields (regarded by specialists as infrastructural) will positively stimulate cooperative efforts in various sectors of economics, trade and industry.

The magnitude and complexity of these problems call for far-reaching and responsible decisions which can be taken at the appropriately high inter-governmental level. That could be the task of the all-European inter-state conferences we are proposing. As is known, the practical aspects of holding an all-European meeting on the environment are being examined within the ECE, where interest has also been shown in the possibility of convening high-level conferences on the two other subjects – transport and energy.

We believe that the Belgrade Meeting can and must contribute to the furtherance of that constructive initiative, which is fully in line with the spirit and letter of the Final Act. We hope that the participating states will approach this matter in a business-like manner free from political bias. A concerted solution of those global problems on the European continent might in future serve as a pattern for their solution on a world scale.

Mr. Chairman, the Helsinki Conference chartered guidelines for equal economic cooperation in Europe. Today we can note with satisfaction that appreciable headway has been made here. East-West economic ties have since become broader, deeper and more diversified. The rate of growth of East-West trade has been higher than that of world trade as a whole. Thus, Soviet trade with the West has gone up by 50 per cent in two years.

Industrial cooperation has expanded considerably, particularly in such a new and promising form as buy-back deals. Scientific and technical links have tangibly improved, conditions for business contacts are now better and the volume of economic information has increased.

All this is conducive to the progressive establishment of East-West economic relations on a solid and long-term basis. The results, no doubt, could be even more tangible if all the participating countries equally adhered to the Helsinki accords on the removal of barriers to mutually beneficial trade.

Fruitful results have been reached in developing cooperation in the humanitarian and other fields, which fact of course, promotes peace and mutual understanding among peoples and man's spiritual enrichment. The implementation of the appropriate provisions of the Final Act by all the CSCE states opens up new and wider prospects for greater contacts and cooperation in that field.

We note with satisfaction the recent increase in travel traffic by citizens of European states, including trips on family and other grounds.

The Soviet Union has agreements and educational exchange programmes with almost all the signatory states. More than 44,000 foreign citizens study in our higher educational establishments; every year more than 17,000 Soviet professors, teachers, post graduate and under graduate students go to other countries and the same number of their foreign counterparts are received in the USSR.

Mutual knowledge of one another's languages is an important means of cultural and intellectual communication between the peoples of our countries. The Soviet Union has all the facilities for foreign-language studies. There are two and a half million students of the French language in our country, almost twelve million study English and almost eleven million study German. The Soviet Union for its part readily renders extensive assistance to any country in Russian-language teaching.

Our country attaches great significance to issuing more translated works for the purpose of familiarizing the Soviet reading public with the spiritual values of other peoples. In 1971 about sixty-seven million copies of books by foreign authors were published in the Soviet Union. In 1976 the figure stood at ninety-seven million. Last September Moscow hosted the first international book fair to be held in our country, in which over fifteen hundred publishing houses from sixty-five foreign countries participated. That important event was fully in line with the provisions of the Final Act.

Much still remains to be done in this area. There is a lot of work ahead for all the CSCE countries. In particular, it would be worthwhile to channel attention to the implementation of the provisions of the Final Act concerning the development of international cooperation in the humanitarian and other fields on a multilateral basis. Of course, cooperation in humanitarian as well as in other fields is only feasible on the basis laid down in the Final Act, means strict respect for sovereignty, for the principle of non-interference in internal affairs, for the laws and regulations of every country.

Mr. Chairman, the political will of the participants in the all-European Conference is recorded in the Final Act in the following formula: to act in the interests of peoples, to strive "to improve and intensify their relations and to contribute in Europe to peace, security, justice and cooperation as well as to rapprochement among themselves and with the other states of the world".

The Soviet Union is firmly convinced that the success of the Belgrade meeting could be promoted by a constructive approach in a spirit of cooperation and mutual understanding without prejudicing the political balance of the Helsinki accords. The Final Act as a general programme of action for the signatory states to strengthen peace in Europe should emerge from the Belgrade meeting more deeply rooted in the political soil of Europe. There can be no question of "amending", revising the Final Act, whatever the pretext.

The Soviet delegation proceeds from the assumption that the content of the work of our meeting will be "a thorough exchange of views both of the implementation of the provisions of the Final Act and of the tasks defined by the Conference, as well as, in the context of the questions dealt with by the latter, on the deepening of their mutual relations, the improvement of security and the development of cooperation in Europe, and the development of the process of détente in the future" as unanimously agreed by us all during its preparatory phase.

The Belgrade forum should be a continuation of what was begun in Helsinki; it should be an integral part of the process of détente, should give a fresh impulse to the implementation of the provisions of the Final Act in its entirety and thus become a new step toward greater security and broader cooperation in Europe, as well as promoting the extension of détente to other parts of the world, including the Mediterranean region, which would also be a worthwhile subject for an exchange of views at our meeting.

Stating the Soviet position, the General Secretary of the CPSU Central Committee and President of the Presidium of the USSR Supreme Soviet, L.I. Brezhnev, said:

> "All participating states of the all-European conference have an opportunity to show once again in concrete deeds their good will in connection with the forthcoming meeting in Belgrade. We would like this meeting to be, as originally conceived, a continuation and development of the Helsinki spirit, yet another link in the development of détente. Is this feasible? Yes, it is, provided we prepare ourselves for this meeting and hold it as an act of cooperation rather than of strife. Anyone who tries to turn it in a different direction would be assuming a grave responsibility".

The fact that recently the overwhelming majority of the participating states have clearly expressed themselves in favour of a constructive approach to our work is a guarantee of the success of this meeting.

In conclusion, I would like to say the following. The peoples of Europe have been through the horrors of the two world wars, through the cold war, and still live in the shadow of the danger of nuclear war. They have the legitimate right to live in peace and may provide a good example of making use of that right by building relations between their states on the basis of a lasting peace.

We are confident that the success of our meeting will create a favourable climate for years to come, that it will help to solve fundamental issues of improved security and cooperation in Europe.

Thank you, Mr. Chairman.

OPENING STATEMENT

by *Mr. Graeffe*

MR. GRAEFFE (Belgium) (interpretation from French): Mr. Chairman, distinguished delegates, ladies and gentlemen, allow me first of all to echo the previous speakers and to express, on behalf of the Belgian Government our gratitude to the Yugoslav Government for the hospitality which is making our stay in Belgrade particularly pleasant, and also to offer them our congratulations for the excellent standard of the organization of this meeting in this splendid palace which is the scene of our work.

Belgium is pleased about the results which have been attained by the preparatory meeting. We should like to thank the negotiators who have removed from our path the obstacles which they met last summer, in this way making it possible for us to save precious time.

Mr. Chairman, we have defined détente as being a process of progressively improving relations amongst all our countries. It is a process which we have witnessed for nearly a quarter of a century now and to which we are all deeply attached.

Relations between our countries cover many fields: political, military, economic or humanitarian; these relations also have many different aspects both official and private. Therefore, so that we have true détente we must make sure that it does not neglect any of these fields nor any of these aspects which are all-important.

The Conference on Security and Cooperation in Europe, the Final Act and our meeting in Belgrade which is the follow-up to this are some of the ways in which the process of détente is becoming apparent; this process is also manifested in other multilateral fora and in our bilateral relations too. Nevertheless it remains true that the Final Act and the way in which it is implemented are an essential element of détente. The Conference on Security and Cooperation in Europe and all the countries which participated in it have been subject of minute preparation which took several years and we all remember the obstacles which we had to overcome in order that [it] should meet. The Final Act which crowned the work of the Conference itself involved the efforts of thirty-five delegations for more than two years, delegations which worked indefatigably to prepare the provisions and commitments which would be acceptable to their governments.

The Final Act in which the provisions are stated is not a treaty where provisions of a legal nature would bind their signatories. It is nevertheless a document of considerable political importance. Is it not the fruit of long negotiations during which each sentence, each word were carefully weighed and discussed until the whole was in accordance with the views of us all? Was it not signed by the highest authorities of our thirty-five countries?

This is to highlight the importance which we attach to the Conference on Security and Cooperation in Europe and to the Final Act. We know very well that the tasks which fall to us could not have been carried out overnight and that we have before us a long road to travel, but we also have the Final Act, a lamp to light up the way so that we could avoid pitfalls along the way. Our firm will is to continue our march forward with all the countries participating at this meeting until we have attained the objectives which we have set ourselves.

The Belgrade meeting is the first stage along the way traced out for us by the Final Act. Belgium realizes all the importance of this and hopes it will be fruitful. Belgium will therefore cooperate in everything which will help us make progress. The Signatories of the Final Act have conferred on us as our first mandate to examine jointly and in a thorough manner the implementation of the provisions which they adopted in Helsinki. The Belgrade meeting is not a court which will pass sentence or acquit: our task is to carefully examine progress which has been accomplished over the last two years. Our second mandate is to seek together everywhere where this is necessary means which will make it possible for us to ensure a better application of the Final Act.

This is the desire of Belgium, to see those two mandates carried out scrupulously.

Mr. Chairman, since the Final Act is to guide us in the search which we will undertake in order to try to improve security and cooperation in Europe, I would like, rapidly, to [go] through the provisions and to indicate in passing, on the one hand eye-judgment of the results which have been obtained two years after the signing of the Final Act, and on the other hand, fields in which we feel that improvements are possible.

If we look first of all at the chapter of the Final Act devoted to questions concerning security in Europe, and more particularly the principles, we could say that the thirty-five signatory countries have tried in their mutual relations to conform to these principles and I think we can be pleased that Europe has remained a continent of peace.

We regard as being of equal success, the treaty of Osimo, the agreements concluded between the Federal Republic of Germany and Poland, the Balkan cooperation and the development of relations between the EEC and the non-participating Mediterranean countries.

Belgium, however, feels that we can do even better. If the principles set out in the Final Act are all of primordial importance and must be implemented equally and without reservation, there is one in which Belgian public opinion, like public opinion in many participating states, is particularly interested: I mean the principle of respecting human rights, and fundamental rights, and freedoms. I am sure we did not expect spectacular progress in this field, therefore Belgium will not give way to disappointment, but believes that it is up to us to take very serious stock of the way in which this principle has been implemented.

At the end of this examination, Belgium feels that it would be in conformity with the Final Act if we try all together, taking into account our different political, economic and social systems to find means to ensure a better implementation of this principle. My country, for its part, is ready to contribute to the search for this means, and the implementation for such means.

Of course, as I have already said, we attach equal importance to all the principles and we are open to all proposals which will tend to facilitate or to improve implementation.

Belgium considers military aspects of security as being an essential element of security. Like many other European countries, Belgium is concerned with the meagre results attained during the negotiations in other fora and hopes that these negotiations rapidly lead to agreements which will constitute real progress in this field. We feel, however, that problems which are linked to arms control and disarmament, because of their great complexity, fall outside the terms of reference of this meeting, and it is up to other meetings to solve such problems. It is of course possible to believe that certain people are not wrong when they remind us that it is difficult to talk about security in Europe, as long as the military situation remains as it is on our continent. We could certainly, however, reverse this tenent and say that any progress in the field of disarmament depends in the final analysis on the political will of countries participating at this meeting. This is what gives their full import to the confidence-building measures provided for in the Final Act, measures which are to a certain extent, the interface between these two proposals; although modest from a technical point of view, they testify to our political will to make progress and not to ignore military aspects of security.

We feel that these measures could be improved, and we would be very pleased if they were improved.

Cooperation in the fields of economics, science and technology and environment occupy an important place in the Final Act. Everyone knows that it is exactly in this field that Belgium and its partners in the European Economic Community have transferred to the Community certain of the powers which were in their hands before the signing of the Treaty of Rome.

One of the main objectives which the member States of the EEC set for themselves in signing the Treaty of Rome in 1958, was to contribute by their future actions to the development of world trade. They were convinced, as they still are, that trade is a dynamic element in the economic progress of all peoples and in this way contributes to the consolidation of peace in the world.

The European Economic Community, which is the world's largest trading block, cannot be a closed entity. It is closely linked to the rest of the world both because of its sources of supply and because of its market. Therefore it can only have one wish, that is, to see harmonious progress year by year in its economic relations with all the signatories of the Final Act. It has not spared and will not spare any effort to make this so. It was also convinced that the principle of reciprocity making it possible for fair distribution of advantages and obligations as stated in the general preamble of this chapter, constitutes an adequate basis for achieving new progress.

The same thing is true of relations between the EEC and all the other countries in the world with whom it has ties of solidarity. Its vocation is to contribute as far as it is able, to the economic development of less advantaged countries in order to reduce economic disparities which exist in the world. It has shown by its actions over the last few years that that was its intention. During the last few years, despite economic difficulties of one kind or another which have not spared any of the signatory countries of the Final Act, economic cooperation between these countries has still developed. Studies carried out in the context of the Economic Commission for Europe of the United Nations have contributed to promote this development. Relatively satisfactory results which we have obtained are a good augury for the future and should encourage us to obtain even better results.

We attach great interest to the provisions of the Final Act which refer to security and cooperation in the Mediterranean. The many links which we have with these countries encourage us to seek with them in this forum means to strengthen this cooperation. We are therefore interested to hear the contributions which will be made to our discussion by the distinguished delegates of States from the South Mediterranean.

Touching on the vast subject of cooperation in the humanitarian field, fields of culture and education, I would like to say at the outset that this is a subject which is particularly dear to us. We are convinced that more free contacts between the nationals of our countries and a broader and more free dissemination of ideas [as] signs of greater reciprocal trust are an essential element in détente as we see it, this is détente which is not just applied at the level of inter-state relations, but also the level of relations between individuals.

We also believe that it is these very fields which at the present time offer us prospects of progress which are the most worth exploring. We certainly recognize the fact that a certain amount of progress has been achieved, over the last two years which have elapsed since the signing of the Final Act and that in particular contacts between nationals of our countries have been facilitated to a certain extent. Neither will we forget that the programme proposed to us by the Final Act is a long-term programme and we could not expect it to be accomplished in two years. However, a great deal remains to be done and we are convinced that we can, by mutually respecting our institutions, work together so that men and ideas can circulate more freely between our countries so that the compartments in which we find ourselves become less water-tight in the future.

In adopting this approach we will only of course be conforming to the provisions of the Final Act. We therefore should persevere in the path which has been indicated to us and we hope that this meeting will stimulate our efforts in the years to come.

We also attach appropriate importance to cooperation and exchange in the fields of culture and education; we are particularly pleased at the work which has been carried out in this field under the aegis of UNESCO. I would, however, like to say, that as far as we are concerned, different manifestations of the creative power of man which we call culture, is not the property of the State, but is the property of creative individuals. The State can only play a complimentary role in the cultural field. It is an important role but it is not the determining role. We therefore believe that in order to be fruitful, cultural cooperation should above all encourage contacts between these creative spirits which are the very substance of our cultures. The Final Act encourages us to do this and we hope, here, too, that progress will be achieved.

Mr. Chairman, from the 1st July up to the 31st December of this year, Belgium has assumed the Chairmanship of the European Communities. European Communities are a fundamentally dynamic institution and their vocation is to achieve in the relatively near future unity amongst its partners in ever broadening spheres.

Member States of the Communities are deeply convinced that the progress that they are achieving will make it possible for them to contribute more effectively to constructive dialogue in Europe and in the world and in this way will promote development of cooperation with all countries.

Therefore, it is not surprising that the ideas which I have had the honour to express do not just reflect the ideas of my country, but also the ideas of the other members of the Communities. I would recall in this respect that the Council of Ministers of the Community authorized two years ago its president in office, President Moro to sign the Final Act in Helsinki on behalf of the European Community.

Certain distinguished delegates of countries from the European Communities have had the opportunity to express their ideas before me and others will have the opportunity to speak after me. You will find in different forms the same solid pattern of arguments, which my delegation, because of the role that is evolved to Belgium, over this six months, will have the opportunity to recall on behalf of the European Community during the discussions of this meeting.

In conclusion, please allow me to confirm the determination of the European Communities to implement all the provisions of the Final Act and, in all these fields, to contribute as much as possible to the strengthening of security and cooperation in Europe, the very objectives for which we have met today.

OPENING STATEMENT

by *Mr. Dobrosielski*

MR. DOBROSIELSKI (Poland):
Mr. Chairman, Distinguished Delegates, Ladies and Gentlemen, first of all I should like to associate myself with previous speakers in expressing our gratitude and appreciation to the Government of Yugoslavia, a country with which Poland maintains the friendliest of relations. Our hosts have made tremendous efforts to create excellent conditions and the right atmosphere for our work.

We are most grateful to the President of Yugoslavia, Marshal Josip Broz Tito, for his good wishes and words of encouragement. We shall, all of us, I have no doubt, bear them in mind in our search for common solutions to ensure that our Belgrade Meeting is crowned with full success.

Mr. Chairman, the two years which have elapsed since the solemn signing of the Final Act at Helsinki are too short a period of time for a full assessment of the influence which the results of the CSCE have exerted and are continuing to exert on the development of the situation in Europe. It is however, already possible to affirm that the Helsinki Conference has yielded positive results. Peace in Europe has been strengthened. The apprehension of an immediate military threat has been reduced and the forms of political and other consultations have been enriched and expanded. Economic, scientific and technoligical and cultural cooperation has been intensified, as has been cooperation in the spheres of education, information and human contacts. It is true that even more progress could and should have been achieved and that the programme laid down in the Final Act should have been more rapidly and efficiently implemented so that some of the criticisms voiced by previous speakers are perhaps understandable. Nevertheless, if we look objectively at the state of relations among the participating countries and compare it with the state of those relations say, ten or fifteen years ago we cannot fail to see how much the situation has changed for the better.

It is clear that the CSCE has not radically changed the situation in Europe overnight and no realistically-minded person could have expected that to happen. Europe is still a region in which, while there are many factors, notably the results of the CSCE, favourable to the comprehensive development and consolidation of the process of détente, some factors of an adverse character remain to be eliminated. The heritage of the Cold War, the division into opposing military blocs, the arms race, the suspicion, the artificial barriers impeding economic cooperation, could not be, and could not have been expected to be liquidated by a single conference or a single document.

It is not our intention in this brief statement to enumerate all the positive results stemming from the implementation of the Final Act or to draw attention to all the negative factors that still exist in Europe. Nor do we intend to engage in polemics regarding behaviour which may not always have been consistent with the letter and spirit of the Final Act. What we should like to do is to indicate, as concisely as possible, Poland's approach to the problems of European security and to the implementation of the provisions of the Final Act.

Mr. Chairman, one of the basic premises of the Polish People's Republic's foreign policy has always been that the security of Poland is indivisible from that of Europe as a whole and that the division of Europe into hostile political and military groupings must be put to an end. It was this premise that underlay our proposal for the establishment of a nuclear-free zone in Central Europe, or, failing that, for the freezing of nuclear armaments in that region. It also underlay the proposal we made on 14 December 1964, at the 19th session of the United Nations General Assembly, for the convening of a Conference on European Security. It was one of the premises underlying the active efforts we made, in conjunction with our friends and allies, to make the holding of the CSCE possible by creating the appropriate conditions, among other things, through the conclusion of a treaty concerning the normalization of our relations with the Federal Republic of Germany. Finally, it was this premise that led us to play an active and constructive part in the detailed preparations for the CSCE and in the actual work of the Conference, and that leads us today to seek to play a similar part in promoting the full implementation of the provisions of the Final Act, which we regard as one of the principal tasks of Polish foreign policy.

Mr. Chairman, the results achieved by the CSCE at Helsinki were received with great satisfaction and considerable optimism in Poland. We see them as evidence of an historic transformation in the quality of the relations among the participating states, as a symbol of the ending of the Cold War period and as a pledge of the definite and universal acceptance and recognition of the territorial and socio-political realities that emerged in Europe as the result of the victory over fascism in the Second World War, of the Potsdam decisions and of subsequent developments. We consider that the decisions of the Final Act, which apply, to all intents and purposes, to all domains of international relations, embody whatever has been found to be positive and useful in the past and provide the basis for a programme of peaceful European development for decades to come.

The provisions of the Final Act are implemented by Poland unilaterally, bilaterally and multilaterally, as the Act requires. On the *unilateral* level, all government institutions and organs are required to respect, observe and implement the provisions of the Final Act. To this end, a comprehensive programme has been drawn up and is being implemented by the various bodies concerned, under the overall supervision of the Minister for Foreign Affairs. I should like to stress that this programme is designed to ensure Poland's implementation of the provisions of the Final Act and not to monitor their implementations by other States.

On the *bilateral* level, since Helsinki, Poland has concluded a number of new agreements with various participating states, expanding our cooperation with them in many fields. Particularly noteworthy are the relations between Poland and France, which for years have been an example of cooperation between states with different socio-political systems. Edward Gierek's recent visit to France and the results of his talks with President Giscard d'Estaing symbolize this cooperation. The joint Franco-Polish declaration, signed during that visit, expresses the hope that our present Meeting will fulfil its task and will contribute to the tangible and dynamic implementation of the Final Act, thus strengthening the process of détente. Poland's relations with the Nordic countries and with many other Western states are also developing favourably.

Our recent agreements with the Federal Republic of Germany have also contributed to the cause of détente and security in Europe, and it is almost symbolic that these agreements were hammered out during the negotiations held by the leaders of the two countries in Helsinki, immediately after the signing of the Final Act.

On the *multilateral* level, we, together with our friends, take numerous constructive initiatives both at the United Nations and in many other international organizations and conferences. In November 1976, the States Parties to the Warsaw Treaty, meeting in Bucharest, presented concrete and highly significant proposals in a document concerning new perspectives in international détente, the strengthening of security and the development of cooperation in Europe. The distinguished representatives of Romania, Bulgaria, Czechoslovakia and the Soviet Union have already drawn attention to these proposals. My delegation associates itself unreservedly with their remarks.

Mr. Chairman, the main factor defining international relations in Europe is the existence, on our continent, of states with different political, social and economic systems. This fact has long been recognized in realistic socio-political circles as a permanent element shaping the development of Europe. In this situation, the adoption of the principle of peaceful coexistence in relations between participating states is not only possible but absolutely necessary.

The Declaration of Principles included in the Final Act is, in our view, a concrete, realistic and systematic codification of the principles of peaceful coexistence between states as those principles apply to the conditions existing in contemporary Europe. Its realism and its balanced character derive precisely from the fact that it was jointly worked out by all the States taking part in the CSCE.

It is worth recalling that in the Final Act, the participating states undertook to, and I quote "respect each other's right freely to choose and develop its political, social, economic and cultural systems as well as its right to determine its laws and regulations".

The Declaration of Principles taken as a whole contains all the necessary elements for the maintenance of lasting peace for the creation of a lasting system of security and cooperation, provided, however, that it is respected and implemented as a whole and not selectively. This means:

Firstly, the adoption, as a fundamental condition and premise for peace on our continent, of *full recognition and observance* of existing territorial and political realities in Europe. This finds expression in the principles of sovereign equality, inviolability of frontiers, territorial integrity of states, and equal rights and self-determination of peoples.

Secondly, the avoidance of actions infringing those basic premises for peace and security in Europe, in other words, the *observance* of the principles of refraining from the threat or use of force and of non-intervention in internal affairs.

Thirdly, the active *implementation and application* of principles which contribute to the building and consolidation of peace and security, such as peaceful settlement of disputes, respect for human rights and fundamental freedoms, cooperation among states, and fulfilment in good faith of obligations under international law.

It is only through the observance and practical application of all ten principles that the results of the Conference can be made fully effective.

Full, unfailing and active observance of all ten principles by all the participating states in their mutual dealings would do a very great deal to strengthen the foundation of peace, security, justice, social progress and mutually advantageous cooperation in Europe.

This is how we in Poland interpret the significance of the Declaration of Principles. We recognize and respect all of them. We adhere to and actively implement and apply them and we do this both at the governmental and the non-governmental level.

We note with pleasure that no one any longer openly questions these principles. What is more, they have been reaffirmed in many bilateral instruments, joint declarations, communiqués and other documents concluded among participating States. Poland itself has concluded such instruments with France, the United States of America, the Federal Republic of Germany, the United Kingdom, Canada, Sweden, Belgium, the Netherlands, Austria, Portugal, Norway and other countries.

Mr. Chairman, for some time now, the question of human rights has received a great deal of attention in the mass media and in political speeches, especially as our Meeting in Belgrade has drawn nearer. It has also been mentioned by previous speakers during this debate. More often than not, however, there is a tendency for the principle in question, Principle 7, concerning respect for human rights and fundamental freedom, to be considered in isolation, without reference to the context of all ten principles in which it belongs. It is worth recalling at this point that Principle 7 speaks of civic, political, economic, social, cultural and other rights.

The right to live, to live in peace and security, is the most elementary human right. The implementation of this is of absolutely basic importance, for it conditions the possibility of enjoying all other rights, not only civic and political but economic, social and cultural rights as well. That is why we are of the opinion that whoever is *really* in favour of human rights must support first and foremost the policy of peace, security and international cooperation. The years of détente in Europe have expanded the sphere of human rights and fundamental freedoms for millions and millions of people all over Europe.

Acting on this principle, Poland ratified, on 3 March this year, the International Human Rights Covenants. In many respects Polish legislation has gone considerably further than the Covenants require. The amnesty decreed by the Council of State last July – the eighth in the postwar period – is striking evidence of our state's attitude. In our respect for human rights and fundamental freedoms, we are guided by the lofty traditions of our nation in its fight for liberty and progress, and by the humanist ideals of socialism.

On 30 June this year, Edward Gierek, speaking in the Polish Parliament, said

> We Poles, communists and citizens of a socialist country, cannot fail to take a sincere and profound interest in humanitarian problems. It was under no other banner than the banner on which the elementary human rights were inscribed that we continued fighting, during so many decades, for national freedom and social justice.

Mr. Chairman, Poland engages in systematic activities aimed at facilitating and enlarging international economic cooperation, scientific and technological collaboration and cooperation in other fields on the principle of equality and without any discrimination. A number of regulations have been issued in Poland which make it easier for foreign commercial organizations and enterprises to carry on their business and for foreign legal and physical persons to engage in economic activity on Polish territory.

Further unilateral steps have been taken to facilitate and simplify tourism in order to promote its development. These unilateral Polish measures to facilitate the development of human contacts are very often not reciprocated. We are, therefore, all the more satisfied that among the ten countries with which we have concluded agreements to abolish visas are Austria, Finland and Sweden, in addition, of course, to the socialist states. We have always been prepared to conclude similar agreements with other countries which are interested.

Poland is pursuing an active policy in order to improve dissemination of, and access to, information. We have worked out a variety of original ways of giving Polish citizens access to the foreign press, both from the West and from the East.

The scope of the cooperation and exchange undertaken by Poland in the field of culture and education is so large, and I hope, so well known, that there is no need for me to dwell on it now; it goes far beyond the framework and arrangements adopted in the Final Act.

Mr. Chairman, we attach great importance to the need to spread knowledge of the results of the CSCE among the population. This is reflected in publications of various types and documents, as well as in the introduction of the problems of the CSCE as a subject in school curricula and various types of adult education.

Education in the spirit of the CSCE is treated by us as an important element in the process of bringing nations closer together, building confidence among nations and teaching respect for the achievements and values contributed by every nation to the common heritage of mankind.

I would like to stress strongly at this point the enormous efforts and accomplishments of the Polish educational and scientific authorities in the field of *education for peace*, from primary school to university and adult education. The Polish delegation will dwell at greater length on this topic in the further work of our Meeting.

Mr. Chairman, the CSCE was the outcome of the policy of détente, the gradual acceptance of the principles of peaceful coexistence and the transition from confrontation to negotiation and cooperation. Those circles that were and remain opposed to détente still spare no effort to hamper and frustrate this process, to sow distrust and to minimize the importance of the results of the CSCE.

In Helsinki, we jointly adopted the rules of conduct that should govern our mutual relations. We are jointly learning to apply them in practice. We are jointly gaining experience. We now have the opportunity to consider jointly how to consolidate, expand and deepen the positive results and how to eliminate adverse phenomena which occur in relations among our states.

Poland, like the other socialist states, will continue to strive to ensure that realism and common sense prevail at the Belgrade Meeting, to ensure that the common interest of all the states and nations participating, the interests of peace, international security, cooperation beneficial to all, justice and social progress will win.

"Our objective is", as Edward Gierek stated in Helsinki, "to make it possible for the people of Poland, Europe and the whole world, to live in peace, freedom and security, dignity and prosperity".

Mr. Chairman, we should like to have not only a deeper exchange of views and experience concerning the implementation of the Final Act and the tasks mapped out by the Helsinki Conference with all the participants. We should also like to consider together how to implement the provision of the Act better and more concretely and how to follow up our joint activities constructively in the future. We should like to see our Belgrade Meeting provide the new impetus that is now so needed in order to consolidate and extend the process of détente.

Thank you very much, Mr. Chairman.

OPENING STATEMENT

by *Mr. Minić*

MR. MINIĆ (Socialist Federal Republic of Yugoslavia) (interpretation from Serbo-Croat):
Mr. Chairman, distinguished representatives of participating states, ladies and gentlemen, comrades, I feel particularly honoured and gratified to extend today, at the outset of the work of the Belgrade Meeting of the Conference on Security and Cooperation in Europe, on behalf of the Federal Executive Council, a most cordial welcome to all the participants in this gathering. I wish to express, at the same time, the satisfaction of Yugoslavia, as host and participating State, at the successful outcome of the Preparatory Meeting. This success has enabled us to embark upon this new phase of multilateral consultations in which, I am certain, all of us will make the utmost efforts to promote and strengthen the process of cooperation and security in Europe.

This Meeting is taking place in an international situation characterized by difficulties regarding détente, which could jeopardize many of the results achieved so far with regard to the democratization of international relations, unless such a state of affairs is rapidly overcome. Crises in the Middle East, in Cyprus and elsewhere are not solved, while new crises are also arising. There is a procrastination regarding the liquidation of the remnants of colonialism, racism and apartheid in southern Africa. There is no real progress towards the establishment of the new international economic order. We are witnesses to some cases of interference in the internal affairs of other countries and recourse to a policy of pressure and force with all the dangerous consequences inherent in such a policy. Nor have the initial steps been taken in the field of disarmament, while the arms race is gaining in intensity and becoming ever more dangerous. There are numerous other problems as well.

At the same time, peoples and countries are aspiring more and more towards full independence, sovereignty, territorial integrity, the right to chart themselves the course of their internal development and to be equal, active and respected members of the international community.

At the same time, there are broad international action and efforts – true, still insufficient – to find peaceful solutions to urgent international problems.

These developments characterize the present moment in the development of international relations, which has been very clearly manifested in the general debate and other activities now taking place at the thirty-second session of the General Assembly of the United Nations.

The situation in our continent is, of course, a component part of international relations. The interrelatedness and interdependence of developments in Europe and in other regions of the world make it even more imperative to exert efforts towards the process of relaxation of international tensions becoming universal. It is ever more obvious that world problems cannot be solved successfully within a narrow circle of countries, nor on bloc bases, but only through the endeavours of all the members of the international community and in accordance with the principles of peaceful coexistence.

Mr. Chairman, distinguished delegates, we are faced with an important and responsible task arising out of the Final Act of the Conference on Security and Cooperation in Europe, which was signed by the Heads of State or Government of our states, committing thereby the governments of all our countries to make their full contribution to the realization of the principles and provisions embodied in this historic document. We are now undertaking this task on the basis of the mandate deriving from the Final Act.

Although a period of a little more than two years is not sufficient for implementing all the provisions contained in the Final Act which, actually, constitutes a long-term platform for the promotion of relations and cooperation in Europe, it nevertheless enables us to sum up the results achieved and the experiences acquired and to take further steps towards accelerating the implementation of the provisions of the Final Act. We consider that the results achieved so far with regard to the application of the provisions of the Final Act on the universal, bilateral and multilateral plane have confirmed beyond any doubt the soundness and lasting value of this document with respect to the development of relations among European countries and international relations in general. We may note with satisfaction that – since Helsinki – the states participating in the Conference on Security and Cooperation in Europe have adopted, on the whole, a constructive attitude towards the obligations assumed by them.

We feel that notable results, which should not at all be underestimated have been achieved with regard to the implementation of the provisions of the Final Act in the course of the last two years.

In our view, among the most important results in this respect are the Agreements of Osimo on the settlement of border and other issues, concluded between Yugoslavia and Italy. These agreements provide a positive example showing that it is possible to solve disputes under the conditions of the existence of good will, of patient negotiations, full equality and respect for mutual interests. We believe that the Agreement of Osimo provide a good example of implementation of the Final Act and constitute an important contribution to the stabilization of conditions, of peace, security and the development of international cooperation in Europe and in the world at large. Prominent, in this respect, also is the role played by the agreements concluded, after Helsinki, between the Federal Republic of Germany and the People's Republic of Poland and some other agreements. We consider that initial steps towards promoting cooperation in the Balkans, too, represent an effort of Balkan countries which is worthy of attention and is aimed at implementing the provisions of the Final Act of the Conference on Security and Cooperation in Europe in this region where our country is also situated.

However, I believe that we all agree that the results achieved are not commensurate either with the possibilities or with the needs of member countries or, for that matter, with the expectations of the public opinions of Europe and of the world. I am convinced, therefore, that we have all come to this Meeting with a sufficient measure of good will and readiness to do our utmost to ensure a more consistent and intensive application of assumed obligations.

We consider that this Meeting should thoroughly appraise the extent to which the provisions of the Final Act have been implemented. We favour an open debate oriented toward concrete measures liable to promote European security and cooperation. Yugoslavia has been consistently striving for a gradual abatement of divisions and differences, both in the field of political and economic and in that of humanitarian issues, and feels that our debate should devote full attention to the implementation of all the sections of the Final Act, that is, integral implementation of this document. In this connexion we find it quite natural and understandable that every one of our countries – depending on general and on its own specific interests – will devote, in the debate, greater or lesser attention to some particular problems. In this regard, my country's delegation, too, will devote special attention to certain issues.

Mr. Chairman, Yugoslavia has always maintained that the foundation of European security can be solid and lasting only if efforts towards relaxation of tensions in the sphere of political relations are accompanied by corresponding measures in the military sphere. This idea of complementarity of political and military aspects of European security has been incorporated into the text of the Final Act of the Conference on Security and Cooperation in Europe. We are now faced with the obligation to consolidate the first modest steps we have taken in that sense and to complement them with new, more substantive and comprehensive measures aimed at strengthening security and mutual confidence.

The existing confidence-building measures, such as, for instance, the notification of major military manoeuvres – whose significance we appreciate and which we consistently implement – should be extended to other fields of military activity of states as well. Otherwise, the number of notified manoeuvres will increase, whereas the aim towards which we are tending is the reduction, and not the increase, of the role of the military factor in relations among European States.

There has been not only a lack of progress with regard to the reduction of armaments and armed forces, about which negotiations are conducted outside the framework set by the Final Act, but the situation has even deteriorated in some areas. The problems of reduction of armaments and disarmament are of vital importance to all European peoples and countries and their successful solution would contribute towards setting in motion a process of disarmament which is the most important task of our time. For this reason we attach exceptional significance to the forthcoming special session of the General Assembly of the United Nations devoted to disarmament. Special responsibility in this regard is borne by the states participating in the Conference on Security and Cooperation in Europe, in the territories of which is found the greatest concentration of military forces and armaments. It goes without saying, therefore, that consideration of the military aspects of European security is an exceptionally important part of the mandate of the Belgrade Meeting, embodied in the Final Act.

May I quote, in connexion with the problems of disarmament, the following passage from the speech delivered by the President of the Socialist Federal Republic of Yugoslavia, Josip Broz Tito, at the Helsinki Conference: "Unless decisive steps towards reducing armed forces and armaments, that is, towards disarmament, are taken, the results of the policy of détente achieved so far might be jeopardized."

The unstable situation in the Mediterranean, a region inseparably linked to Europe, makes it incumbent on us to exert concerted efforts along the line of decisions embodied in the Final Act. In spite of a positive evolution with regard to the indentification of crucial problems, the situation in the Mediterranean has deteriorated in many respects. We are also convinced that the non-European Mediterranean countries also will contribute toward the Belgrade Meeting not only continuing, but also deepening the joint dialogue with regard to all questions concerning security and the promotion of cooperation in the Mediterranean, as a component of security and cooperation in Europe.

A constant advancement of economic, humanitarian, cultural and scientific relations is also significant for the consolidation of peace, security and development of all-round cooperation among all the States participating in the Conference on Security and Cooperation in Europe. We believe that attainment of results in one field should not be made conditional on a situation in another field.

A considerable growth of economic cooperation among the participating states, particularly in the field of trade, has been noted during the last few years. A dynamic implementation of the conclusions of the Final Act is now in course, especially of those that are of a multilateral character, the United Nations Economic Commission for Europe (ECE) playing an important role in this regard. Yugoslavia is of the opinion that the said Organization should be enabled to play a more substantive role in the development of mutual economic cooperation, as this offers, in our mind, the possibility of gradually overcoming phenomena of coercion and discrimination in trade and tendencies to subordinate the implementation of the provisions of the Final Act to the interests of some states or economic-political groupings, to the detriment of the small and less developed countries of Europe.

We believe that, in solving European economic problems, we must constantly bear in mind the fact that the European economy forms part of world economy and that any solution that would fail to take this into account and, especially, fail to take into consideration the interests of the developing countries, would be bound to exert a negative influence on Europe as well. The role of the countries participants in the Conference on Security and Cooperation in Europe is all the greater as the negotiations now in course between the developed and the developing countries concerning the solution of key world economic problems are going through a period of serious crisis. We believe that the Declaration adopted by one hundred and fourteen developing countries belonging to the Group of 77, at their meeting held in New York on the level of Ministers of Foreign Affairs on September 29, 1977, will provide a new incentive for the continuation of negotiations. We hope that the thirty-second session of the General Assembly of the United Nations will adopt appropriate and concrete decisions for the continuation of these negotiations and for a more rapid solution of the most acute international economic problems, in particular, along the line of establishment of the new international economic order.

We also believe that the realization of human rights should be constantly promoted through all-round equal cooperation. Yugoslavia feels that the question of the realization of human rights should be approached in a comprehensive manner and considered with a full measure of responsibility and realism, all this with a view to ensuring the constant implementation and further improvement of the provisions of the Final Act in this field. In our opinion, the problem of human rights cannot be isolated from historical, political, economic, social, cultural and other circumstances, which are different in every country.

An inseparable element of human rights is also the free expression of national culture and use of one's own language and writing: this must apply, of course, to all nations and not only to national minorities.

I would like to emphasize, on this occasion, that the equality of nations and nationalities in my country, in Yugoslavia, has become a constitutional and real social relationship, that is, the foundation of the Yugoslav federal, socialist and self-managing community where the freedom of one nation or nationality is simultaneously a condition for the freedom of all. In view of this, it is easy to understand why Yugoslavia has been insisting consistently on the necessity to devote full attention to the problem of national minorities.

This time also, we shall uphold the view that the problem of the status of minorities and groups is not merely a domestic issue concerning any given country, but is also of vital importance to the strengthening of security and promotion of good-neighbourly relations and cooperation among countries. This meeting of the Conference on Security and Cooperation in Europe should review the results of the implementation in the provisions of the Final Act relating to the question of minorities and make a further contribution towards its solution.

Further progress in the sphere of the so-called "third basket" will depend on the establishment of equitable relations and on better mutual acquaintance among European peoples and countries. The weakening of monopoly in the spheres of information, culture and transfer of scientific and other knowledge will greatly contribute to this, as such a monopoly affects negatively the cultures of smaller countries.

Mr. Chairman, distinguished delegates, ladies and gentlemen, comrades, we consider that the Conference on Security and Cooperation is the most important result achieved, in Europe, in the field of détente, security and cooperation based on equal rights and on the sovereign equality of all participating states. Actually, the Conference is part of a broader process of democratization of international relations. Therefore, all attempts at asserting or imposing the narrow interests of some countries, groups of countries or blocs are contrary to the very essence of the Final Act.

Other positive and progressive factors and forces in the world are also striving to strengthen and to expand the process of relaxation of international tensions. One of the most important factors, whose influence in international relations is rapidly expanding, is the movement of non-aligned countries. The developing countries, whose solidarity is constantly growing, are striving toward the same objective, exerting ever more resolute and successful efforts for the establishment of a new international economic order ensuring more equitable international economic relations than those prevailing today and for the development of international economic cooperation based on equal rights, in the interests of all countries, both developed and developing.

The Socialist Federal Republic of Yugoslavia will strive, at the Belgrade Meeting, for the full reassertion of the Final Act and for the continuation of the policy of détente in Europe and more widely. Our activity will be oriented towards the adoption of measures and recommendations liable to accelerate a more complete, comprehensive and dynamic implementation of the conclusions of the Final Act.

In our view, it is very important to oppose tendencies aimed at upsetting the balanced character of the Final Act, at disrupting its integrity and obscuring its precision as well as attempts at diminishing the importance of the continuity of the Conference on Security and Cooperation in Europe. We feel that it is in our common interest to preserve what has already been achieved and to adopt new measures for the further promotion of détente, security and cooperation in Europe. It is our profound belief that this can be achieved if we proceed from the fact that we are an inseparable part of an interrelated and interdependent world and that, consequently, we cannot withdraw into isolation. Nor can we arrogate to ourselves the right to behave differently toward other countries and peoples than we behave in the relations among the countries we represent here, expecting to preserve in this way a privileged position and to be spared from the difficulties and crises affecting countries and regions on other continents. It is essential, therefore, that we should base our relations with other countries in the world on the same principles that we wish to apply for further developing European security and cooperation and that we should strive for solving those global international problems on the solution of which progress on our continent depends.

Distinguished participants in this very important Belgrade Meeting, negotiations in such a forum are a complex affair. Possible difficulties and stagnation in its work are a normal phenomenon which should not be dramatized. At this gathering we are all equally responsible for its work and its outcome. We are, however, certain that our deliberations will be crowned with success, provided all the participants exert utmost efforts and provided there is a political will to achieve success.

Today, we are continuing substantive political talks on the broadest basis offered by the Final Act. We are convinced that, as a result of this Meeting, peace, security and cooperation in Europe will be further strengthened on the basis of the principles adopted by the Conference on Security and Cooperation in Europe. It is, at the same time, the best contribution that we can make to the cause of peace, security and cooperation in the world in general.

Thank you, Mr. Chairman.

OPENING STATEMENT

by *Mr. Leifland*

MR. LEIFLAND (Sweden):
Mr. Chairman, may I join with earlier speakers in thanking the Government of Yugoslavia for their willingness in acting as host for this Meeting. I also want to thank the Government of Yugoslavia for the splendid way in which the preparatory meeting was carried out. I am convinced that the practical organization of this Main Meeting will be of equal excellence.

Sweden regards the choice of Belgrade for this meeting as a recognition of the important role Yugoslavia, by virtue of its policy of nonalignment, plays on the international scene.

Mr. Chairman, the Conference on Security and Cooperation was the result of the state of affairs prevailing in Europe after World War II. The situation after the war did not lead to normal relations between the states in Europe. The differences between social systems were far too great.

Stability was built on the balance of arms, not on respect and confidence. This situation created by the war, remains in many respects unchanged. Huge weapon arsenals and combat-ready forces, rather than trustful cooperation, are all too often considered to be the primary guarantors of peace.

But the absurdity of trying to build lasting peace on a balance of terror has become increasingly obvious. The conviction that it must be possible for nations to live together on a basis other than that of threat of armed forces has grown stronger and stronger.

On the strength of this conviction it has become possible to initiate and strengthen the process we call détente. One of the foundations of détente is the fact that the nuclear powers are aware of the importance of avoiding every situation that could possibly lead to a military confrontation. Another condition necessary for détente was created by the agreements reached between East and West a few years ago concerning the normalization of the situation in Central Europe. Cardinal in this context were the agreements between the two German states.

The fact that the SALT talks do continue, undoubtedly plays an important role in the process of détente. However, I cannot suppress the deep concern felt by the Swedish Government about the build-up of nuclear arsenals and the rapid development of arms technology. This leads to the result that attempts to reach stability are forced up onto ever higher and more dangerous levels of armament. So far, no progress towards genuine disarmament has been made. Against this background, we welcome the statements to the effect that efforts to reach a new and, as we hope, more significant agreement can be expected to yield results in the not too distant future. Such an agreement must then be the starting point for further negotiations aiming at mutual security on a still lower level of armament.

The onset of détente made it possible to start the gradual expansion of economic, scientific and cultural exchange between countries belonging to different social and economic systems. We can perhaps say that the realization of the mutual benefits of those exchanges was an important catalyst in the détente process. The will to continue this cooperation has been confirmed in the Final Act.

Détente, as it looks today is, of course, fragile in many respects. So far, it has in no way been able to take the place of the balance of terror. Nor has progress gone at the rate we have wished. We have regrettably had many setbacks; others might possibly be ahead of us. Détente is not a self-generating process. To continue it requires great efforts and the good will of all those concerned. The driving force, of course, is the simple fact that there is no realistic alternative.

These are some of the facts on which we should base our approach to the CSCE. We made great headway in the work which resulted in the Final Act of the Helsinki Conference more than two years ago, in the summer of 1975. Those efforts were based on the common conviction that war may, and can, no longer be used to attain national goals.

We have agreed upon principles for the conduct of states. Respect for those principles, which are totally congruent with the UN Charter, is an important precondition for a lasting and stable peace.

The Final Act was both an acknowledgment of political realities and a commitment for the future. It confirms certain results achieved that benefit security and cooperation in Europe. At the same time it indicates ways and means to solve problems that have been on the agenda in East-West relations for many, many years.

Some progress has been made in and between our countries in the process of implementing the Final Act. Much more, however, remains to be done. The Final Act has also had a stimulating effect on the work of international organizations. For instance, it has given impetus to the activities of the ECE and been an incentive for new measures to consolidate cooperation in such areas as the environment and the utilization of resources.

It is essential, however, not to be over-optimistic about getting quick results. More than two years are necessary for changing the climate of cooperation between countries with different social systems. The cardinal importance of the Final Act is perhaps that it has given us a foundation to discuss questions of common interest. This means that also issues that divide us can be dealt with in a frank and matter-of-fact way. This discussion in itself establishes contacts and deepens our knowledge so that we learn to understand one another better.

How, then, can we go on building on the foundation which has been laid? How can we deepen détente?

Détente is a concept which has not only military, but also political, cultural, economic, and purely human aspects. Détente must be observed in all those aspects if it is to be really genuine.

We must consolidate the important results already achieved in economic, technological, scientific and cultural fields and vigorously promote this development. The mutual trust patiently built up between persons and institutions active in various fields in our societies must be further strengthened. Cultural cooperation, exchange of information on all the social issues that regard the daily life of individuals, opportunities for mass media to follow the developments in other countries are important elements in this context. This will promote mutual understanding and thus détente.

The economic interdependence has been growing in recent years in spite of the difficult economic situation in Europe. It has brought with it a greater realization of the necessity of increased cooperation.

Mr. Chairman, during the negotiations which led up to the Final Act, the Swedish delegation often had occasion to return to the link between détente and disarmament. Political détente, to enjoy credibility in the eyes of our peoples, must lead to at least some concrete results in disarmament negotiations. When CSCE was initiated, one of the starting points was that the deeper détente in Europe presupposed that concrete results would also be achieved within a reasonable time in the military field. This starting point must be kept constantly in mind. The Vienna talks on force reductions in Central Europe have proved to be very complicated indeed. After several years they have not led to any agreement. The Swedish Government has repeatedly expressed its regrets that no real progress has yet been made. The talks in Vienna very clearly concern the national security of all CSCE states, a fact the Swedish Government has stressed in various contexts.

It has been said that the SALT talks are an important indicator of the willingness of the superpowers to show a sense of responsibility for détente. We certainly share this view. At the same time, however, it must be obvious that a second SALT agreement will not in itself be enough as an impetus for the process of disarmament. This process must contain genuine arms control measures of the type now being discussed, such as a comprehensive test ban treaty, such as the prohibition of chemical warfare.

The particular responsibility resting on the great powers in the disarmament field cannot be over-emphasized. If no results are forthcoming, confidence in the determination to promote peace will be gravely undermined. By effective and genuine disarmament, the parties must demonstrate that they are in earnest about their intention to make this world a safer place to live in.

We all agree that there is a link between disarmament and continuing détente in the spirit of the CSCE. One expression of this is the importance we attach to measures in the military field which can help to eliminate misunderstanding and groundless suspicion. Sweden will at this Conference be presenting a proposal whereby the participating states will gain more benefit from the confidence-building measures.

Mr. Chairman, the Final Act from the Helsinki Conference has had no impact on the basic reasons why there are huge armed forces ready for action in Europe. The mistrust existing between nations is, of course, an expression of deep ideological differences; it also has historical roots. Mistrust is often due to misunderstanding the opposite side's motives and intentions.

The CSCE is a forum where small- and medium-sized states, nonaligned, as well as members of alliances, can voice their opinions on an equal footing.

Sweden's position as a neutral country has made it easier for us to take an active part in international affairs. It is a source of satisfaction to us that the policy of the neutral and the nonaligned countries has gained greater understanding in the world. Not least in the work done under the aegis of the CSCE has their independent position given them valuable opportunities to help solve certain problems.

We are indeed convinced that it is possible to improve cooperation and security to an extent greater than undeniable differences in social systems and historical background perhaps seem to allow. This can be a major task for the CSCE. This does not imply that cooperation between our countries cannot function without the Final Act. It implies rather that, within the framework of the CSCE and with the help of recurrent follow-up meetings, it will be possible to combine respect for the differences in our social and economic systems with an ever increasing exchange of views across our national frontiers. Cooperation between the nations of Europe, just like contacts between its peoples, is an ancient tradition. That tradition should be allowed to continue and develop.

The participating states have given a solemn undertaking in the Final Act not to change frontiers by force. We have declared that we shall respect one another's territorial integrity and that we shall refrain from intervention in one another's internal affairs. Those principles confirm what has already become an established reality in our cooperation. We hope that continued détente and genuine disarmament will so strengthen those principles that none of our societies need fear for safety because of external force.

It cannot be taken for granted that the present pattern of European security will remain unchanged in the long range. We do not want to exclude that one day it will be possible to dismantle the pact system on which our security is based today. This goal may of course seem very remote but it would be absurd and dangerous to get used to regarding it as unattainable.

Mr. Chairman, there have always been differing opinions on how to weigh the demands a state makes on its citizens against the individual's demand for freedom. Not all countries register the wishes of the people in free elections. In our view free debate is an indispensable and desirable part of the development of society. It is regrettable if this natural conflict between the individual and the state is instead regarded as an inner threat to the existence of the state. Such an attitude may also have repercussions on the relationship between nations.

We sincerely hope that with patience and good will we shall be able to eliminate this sense of threat, in the same way as we try to reduce the risk of war. The values held by my country, however, make it impossible to do this by silencing open discussion or by shutting off contacts with other nations. Nations must not cut themselves off from one another because they are afraid. Instead, détente itself should give us scope for an open and free discussion of fundamental political and ideological issues.

The distinguished representative of Norway said yesterday, and I quote: "We on our part are ready to accept criticism from anyone who might disagree with the manner in which we practise the principles laid down in the Final Act". I would like to say for the Swedish Government that we do take exactly the same attitude.

Extended cooperation and contacts in all areas between the peoples of the participating states are, in my Government's view, the course we must choose in order to gradually deepen détente and also prepare the ground for a military disarmament worthy of its name. Here we can get guidance from the provisions of the Final Act.

We are only at the beginning of the work we hope will bring greater clarity and stability to conditions governing relationships between different social systems. The purpose of this meeting, however, is neither to change the Final Act nor to add new provisions to it. We are here to review the implementation and observance of the document in a constructive spirit and to agree on measures to improve security and develop cooperation between us.

The follow-up meeting now convened should be so conducted that future meetings are a natural outcome. All this will be a laborious process that will function best if we avoid confrontation and try to proceed in a constructive way. It is most gratifying that agreement was reached in the summer that this meeting will not end before fixing date and place for a new similar meeting.

The Final Act is a carefully balanced document. Each of its principles must be seen in conjunction with the others. It would be wrong of us here in Belgrade to try and change this balance.

At the same time, it is clear that the Helsinki Act is not just a document without a life of its own. The view has been put forward that two years ago it was possible to agree on this document just because it only laid down accepted realities.

What has happened since 1975 has shown that this view is only partly correct. True, the Security Conference obviously never aimed to force a new social system upon any country. On the other hand, in as much as the Final Act has proved to be a challenging document, it has acquired new dimensions and created new expectations.

In the two years since the Helsinki Conference the Swedish Government and a unanimous public opinion in Sweden have been very concerned about the provisions of the Final Act relating to human rights.

This is only natural. When divided families cannot be reunited, one of the cornerstones of our society is affected. We sympathize deeply with people who are subjected to humiliation and persecution just because they wish to express their views on social and other issues or because they want to practise their religion, or because they want to meet and work together for political or other goals.

The struggle for human rights is not a question of passing moods in public opinion. The conviction that the human being has certain fundamental rights and a unique value is the very essence of democracy.

Every government elected by the people is duty-bound to be

the spokesman for this conviction, even if it implies critizing the conduct of other countries. The Swedish Government will not refrain from drawing attention to violations of human rights. We cannot possibly regard this as interference in the affairs of other nations. The Final Act gives us good grounds for holding this view.

But a government must also carefully consider what best benefits the cause it wants to promote. This is a difficult but not impossible balance to strike.

When discussing human rights we must not forget the broader implication of this concept. If people are to be able to live a life in integrity and dignity we must also recognize their right to employment, to a place to live, to education, to social security and to a decent environment.

Mr. Chairman, representatives of our governments are now discussing in another international forum what can be done to reduce oppression and poverty. The discussions held and the decisions made at the United Nations affect all the countries of the world. A more equitable order in the world cannot be implemented without the solidarity of all those concerned. The thirty-five countries here who represent the rich and industrial world have a particularly heavy responsibility to work for a new international economic order.

But even the results of our work within the framework of the CSCE are of great importance. The safety and security of the world greatly depends on how our mutual relations develop. This imposes an obligation on the participating states here in Belgrade and in their future cooperation.

Mr. Chairman, in conclusion, may I express the hope that our exchange of views during this meeting will be constructive – of benefit to our security and to our cooperation. I want to assure you that the Swedish Government will do its best to promote those goals.

Thank you, Mr. Chairman.

CONCLUDING DOCUMENT

OF THE BELGRADE MEETING 1977 OF REPRESENTATIVES OF THE PARTICIPATING STATES OF THE CONFERENCE ON SECURITY AND COOPERATION IN EUROPE, HELD ON THE BASIS OF THE PROVISIONS OF THE FINAL ACT RELATING TO THE FOLLOW-UP TO THE CONFERENCE

The representatives of the participating states of the Conference on Security and Co-operation in Europe, appointed by the Ministers of Foreign Affairs of these states, met at Belgrade from 4 October 1977 to 9 March 1978 in accordance with the provisions of the Final Act relating to the Follow-up to the Conference.

The participants received a message from the President of the Socialist Federal Republic of Yugoslavia, Josip Broz Tito, and were addressed by Mr. Miloš Minić, Vice-President of the Federal Executive Council and Federal Secretary for Foreign Affairs of the Socialist Federal Republic of Yugoslavia.

Contributions were made by the following non-participating Mediterranean states: Algeria, Egypt, Israel, Lebanon, Morocco, Syria and Tunisia.

The representatives of the participating states stressed the importance they attach to détente, which has continued since the adoption of the Final Act in spite of difficulties and obstacles encountered. In this context they underlined the role of the CSCE, the implementation of the provisions of the Final Act being essential for the development of this process.

The representatives of the participating states held a thorough exchange of views both on the implementation of the provisions of the Final Act and of the tasks defined by the Conference, as well as, in the context of the questions dealt with by the latter, on the deepening of their mutual relations, the improvement of security and the development of co-operation in Europe, and the development of the process of détente in the future.

The representatives of the participating states stressed the political importance of the Conference on Security and Co-operation in Europe and reaffirmed the resolve of their Governments, to implement fully, unilaterally, bilaterally and multilaterally, all the provisions of the Final Act.

It was recognized that the exchange of views constitutes in itself a valuable contribution towards the achievement of the aims set by the CSCE, although different views were expressed as to the degree of implementation of the Final Act reached so far.

They also examined proposals concerning the above questions and the definition of the appropriate modalities for the holding of other meetings in conformity with the provisions of the chapter of the Final Act concerning the Follow-up to the Conference.

Consensus was not reached on a number of proposals submitted to the meeting.

In conformity with the relevant provisions of the Final Act and with their resolve to continue the multilateral process initiated by the CSCE, the participating states will hold further meetings among their representatives. The second of these meetings will be held in Madrid commencing Tuesday, 11 November 1980.

A preparatory meeting will be held in Madrid commencing Tuesday, 9 September 1980, to decide on appropriate modalities for the main Madrid Meeting. This will be done on the basis of the Final Act as well as of the other relevant documents adopted during the process of the CSCE.*

It was also agreed to hold, within the framework of the follow-up to the CSCE, the meetings of experts of the participating states indicated below.

In conformity with the mandate contained in the Final Act and according to the proposal made to this effect by the Government of Switzerland a meeting of experts will be convened at Montreux on 31 October 1978, charged with pursuing the examination and elaboration of a generally acceptable method for peaceful settlement of disputes aimed at complementing existing methods.

Upon the invitation of the Government of the Federal Republic

*The other relevant documents adopted during the process of the CSCE are: The Final Recommendations of the Helsinki Consultations, the Decisions of the Preparatory Meeting to organize the Belgrade Meeting 1977, and this Concluding Document.

of Germany, the meeting of experts envisaged in the Final Act in order to prepare a "Scientific Forum" will take place in Bonn starting on 20 June 1978. Representatives of UNESCO and the United Nations Economic Commission for Europe shall be invited to state their views.

Upon the invitation of the Government of Malta, a meeting of experts on the Mediterranean will be convened on 13 February 1979 in Valletta. Its mandate will be, within the framework of the Mediterranean Chapter of the Final Act, to consider the possibilities and means of promoting concrete initiatives for mutually beneficial co-operation concerning various economic, scientific and cultural fields, in addition to other initiatives relating to the above subjects already under way. The non-participating Mediterranean states will be invited to contribute to the work of this meeting. Questions relating to security will be discussed at the Madrid Meeting.

The duration of the meetings of experts should not exceed 4–6 weeks. They will draw up conclusions and recommendations and send their reports to the Governments of the participating states. The results of these meetings will be taken into account, as appropriate, at the Madrid Meeting.

All the above-mentioned meetings will be held in conformity with paragraph 4 of the chapter on "Follow-up to the Conference" of the Final Act.

The Government of the Socialist Federal Republic of Yugoslavia is requested to transmit the present document to the Secretary-General of the United Nations, to the Director-General of UNESCO and to the Executive Secretary of the United Nations Economic Commission for Europe. The Government of the Socialist Federal Republic of Yugoslavia is also requested to transmit the present document to the governments of the Mediterranean non-participating states.

The representatives of the participating states expressed their profound gratitude to the people and Government of the Socialist Federal Republic of Yugoslavia for the excellent organization of the Belgrade Meeting and the warm hospitality extended to the delegations which participated in the Meeting.

Belgrade, 8 March 1978

REPORT

OF THE MEETING OF EXPERTS REPRESENTING THE PARTICIPATING STATES OF THE CONFERENCE ON SECURITY AND CO-OPERATION IN EUROPE AND THEIR NATIONAL SCIENTIFIC INSTITUTIONS FORESEEN BY THE FINAL ACT OF THE CSCE AND THE CONCLUDING DOCUMENT OF THE BELGRADE MEETING 1977 TO PREPARE THE "SCIENTIFIC FORUM"

In accordance with the provisions of the Final Act of the Conference on Security and Cooperation in Europe and of the Concluding Document of the Belgrade Meeting 1977, the Meeting of Experts representing the participating States and their national scientific institutions, foreseen by the Final Act, took place in Bonn, upon the invitation of the Government of the Federal Republic of Germany, from 20 June to 28 July 1978 in order to prepare a "Scientific Forum".

During the opening session of the meeting the participants were welcomed by Dr. Hildegard Hamm-Brücher, Minister of State, Ministry of Foreign Affairs, on behalf of the Government of the Federal Republic of Germany.

During the first working session representatives of UNESCO and the United Nations Economic Commission for Europe stated their views.

The meeting of experts drew up the following conclusions and recommendations concerning the date, place, duration. Agenda and other modalities of the "Scientific Forum".

The "Scientific Forum" will be held in conformity with the relevant provisions of the Final Act, in the form of a meeting of leading personalities in science from the participating States, in accordance with the intention of the participating States within their competence to broaden and improve cooperation and exchanges in the field of science and thus to continue the multilateral process initiated by the Conference on Security and Co-operation in Europe.

I. Agenda

1. Formal opening of the "Scientific Forum";
Address by a representative of the host country;
Contributions by UNESCO and the United Nations Economic Commission for Europe;
Opening statements by representatives of delegations of the participating States.
2. Discussion of interrelated problems of common interest concerning current and future developments in science, and promotion of expansion of contacts, communications and the exchange of information between scientific institutions and among scientists.
In this context the following areas and subjects shall be considered:
Exact and Natural Sciences
Scientific research, in particular fundamental research, in the fields of alternative energy sources and food production;
Medicine
Current trends in medical research, in particular in basic research and primarily on cardiovascular, tumour and virus diseases, taking into consideration the influence of the changing environment on human health;
The Humanities and Social Sciences
Comparative studies on social, socio-economic and cultural phenomena, especially the problems of human environment and urban development.
3. Closing statements by representatives of delegations of the participating States.
4. Formal closure of the "Scientific Forum".

II. Organizational Framework and Other Modalities

1. The "Scientific Forum" will open on Monday, 18 February 1980 at 10 a.m. in Hamburg, Federal Republic of Germany. Its duration shall be of two weeks.
2. Agenda item 2 will be dealt with in the Plenary and in the appropriate subsidiary working bodies on, respectively, the exact and natural sciences, medicine and the humanities and social

sciences. Other subsidiary bodies may be set up by the Plenary, which is the main body of the "Forum", to deal with specific questions.

3. Agenda items 1, 3 and 4 will be dealt with in open plenary meetings.

4. Invitations to UNESCO and the United Nations Economic Commission for Europe to make their contributions referred to in item 1 of the Agenda will be transmitted by the Executive Secretary.

The Plenary may decide to invite these Organizations to make additional contributions in the appropriate subsidiary working bodies.

5. The opening and closing statements indicated in items 1 and 3 of the Agenda may be made by representatives of delegations of the participating States if they desire to do so. The statements, as a rule, should not exceed 15 minutes per delegation.

6. Contributions pertaining to item 2 of the Agenda may be sent in through the proper channels – preferably not later than three months before the opening of the "Scientific Forum" – to the Executive Secretary, who will circulate them to the other participating States.

7. If the Plenary so decides, the "Forum" may, as a result of its proceedings, draw up recommendations, including such dealing with what further steps might in due course be taken by the participating States of the CSCE with respect to the "Scientific Forum".

The results of the "Forum" may be taken into account, as appropriate, by the participating States at the Madrid Meeting.

8. The Chair at the opening and closing plenary meetings shall be taken by a representative of the delegation of the Federal Republic of Germany. After the opening meeting the Chair shall be taken in daily rotation, in French alphabetical order, starting with a representative of the delegation of Bulgaria.

9. The Government of the Federal Republic of Germany will designate the Executive Secretary of the "Scientific Forum". This designation should be agreed to by the participating States. The services of a technical secretariat will be provided by the host country.

10. Other rules of procedure, working methods and the scale of distribution for the expenses of the CSCE will, *mutatis mutandis*, be applied to the "Scientific Forum".

In addressing itself to Agenda item 2 it is recommended that the "Scientific Forum" should bear in mind present relevant scientific knowledge and goals for future research as well as the present state and future needs of international scientific cooperation, including the education and training of young scientists, interdisciplinary approaches and the different levels of scientific development among participating States.

REPORT

OF THE MEETING OF EXPERTS REPRESENTING THE PARTICIPATING STATES OF THE CONFERENCE ON SECURITY AND CO-OPERATION IN EUROPE FORESEEN BY THE FINAL ACT OF THE CSCE IN ORDER TO PURSUE THE EXAMINATION AND ELABORATION OF A GENERALLY ACCEPTABLE METHOD FOR PEACEFUL SETTLEMENT OF DISPUTES AIMED AT COMPLEMENTING EXISTING METHODS

In accordance with the mandate of the Final Act of the Conference on Security and Co-operation in Europe and the relevant provisions of the Concluding Document of the Belgrade Meeting 1977, a Meeting of Experts representing the participating States took place at Montreux from 31 October to 11 December 1978 in order to pursue the examination and elaboration of a generally acceptable method for peaceful settlement of disputes aimed at complementing existing methods.

At the opening meeting the participants were addressed by Mr. Pierre Aubert, Head of the Federal Political Department, on behalf of the Government of Switzerland.

The participants adopted an agenda and proceeded to a general exchange of views after which several proposals aimed at complementing existing methods for peaceful settlement of disputes were submitted and discussed. A working paper based on the "Draft Convention on a European System for the Peaceful Settlement of Disputes" was submitted for consideration which put forward the following subsidiary and compulsory procedures: negotiation, inquiry, mediation, conciliation and arbitration. Another working paper was submitted for consideration which put forward a proposal of mandatory consultations as a possible method for peaceful settlement of disputes. A further paper was submitted which put forward the concept of a comprehensive method for peaceful settlement of disputes within specific subject areas, including appropriate mandatory features. Other proposals and ideas were put forward for consideration. Divergent views were expressed and no consensus was reached on specific methods.

The participants stressed the importance their governments

attach to détente, which has continued since the adoption of the Final Act in spite of difficulties and obstacles encountered. In this context they underlined the role of the CSCE, the implementation of the provisions of the Final Act being essential for the development of this process.

The participants reaffirmed the adherence of their governments to the principle of peaceful settlement of disputes as enshrined in the Charter of the United Nations and in the Final Act of the CSCE. They also stressed the significance of elaborating, in accordance with the mandate contained in the Final Act, a method for peaceful settlement of disputes.

The participants agreed on a common approach to the elaboration of a method for peaceful settlement of disputes between or among the participating States which should be based on the following:

consistency with the principles and the purposes of the Charter of the United Nations and with the Final Act of Helsinki, especially principle V of the latter document;
consistency with sovereign equality of States, and the free choice of means;
experience and the treaty and diplomatic practice and the views of all the participating States in this field;
acceptability to all participating States irrespective of their political, economic or social systems as well as of their size, goegraphical location or level of economic development;
subsidiarity to existing methods and institutions for the peaceful settlement of international disputes;
complementarity to existing methods so as to promote, in good faith and a spirit of cooperation, a rapid and equitable solution on the basis of international law;
flexibility of the method;
capacity for progressive development of the method.

The method to be elaborated should contribute to peace, security and justice in Europe, to the further development of détente and co-operation among the participating States.

The participants recommended that the participating States consider the possibility of promoting and extending the existing practice of including, in appropriate treaties among and between them, provisions for the peaceful settlement of disputes.

The participants recommended to the governments of States participating in the CSCE that they consider, at the Madrid Meeting, the possibility of convening another Meeting of Experts in order to pursue, on the basis of the Final Act, the examination and elaboration of a generally acceptable method for peaceful settlement of disputes aimed at complementing existing methods, taking into account the common approach set forth above, as well as the various proposals and ideas discussed at the Montreux Meeting.

The participants recommended that contacts between the governments of participating States continue in order better to acquaint themselves with each other's views on the subject of peaceful settlement of disputes.

The participants expressed their deep gratitude to the Government of Switzerland for the excellent organization of the Meeting and for the warm hospitality extended to them during their stay at Montreux.

REPORT

OF THE MEETING OF EXPERTS REPRESENTING THE PARTICIPATING STATES OF THE CONFERENCE ON SECURITY AND CO-OPERATION IN EUROPE, FORESEEN BY THE CONCLUDING DOCUMENT OF THE BELGRADE MEETING 1977 TO CONSIDER, WITHIN THE FRAMEWORK OF THE MEDITERRANEAN CHAPTER OF THE FINAL ACT, THE POSSIBILITIES AND MEANS OF PROMOTING CONCRETE INITIATIVES FOR MUTUALLY BENEFICIAL COOPERATION CONCERNING VARIOUS ECONOMIC, SCIENTIFIC AND CULTURAL FIELDS, IN ADDITION TO OTHER INITIATIVES RELATING TO THE ABOVE SUBJECTS ALREADY UNDER WAY.

1. In accordance with the mandate of the Concluding Document of the Belgrade Meeting 1977, a Meeting of Experts representing the participating States took place at Valletta upon the invitation of the Government of Malta, from 13 February to 26 March 1979 in order to consider within the framework of the Mediterranean Chapter of the Final Act of the Conference on Security and Co-operation in Europe (CSCE), the possibilities and means of promoting concrete initiatives for mutually beneficial co-operation concerning various economic, scientific and cultural fields, in addition to other initiatives relating to the above subjects already under way.

2. During the opening session of the Meeting, a message was received from Dr. Anton Buttigieg, President of the Republic of Malta, and the participants were addressed by Mr. Wistin Abela, Minister of Development, Energy, Port and Telecommunications of the Republic of Malta.

3. The participants adopted an agenda and agreed on modalities appropriate to this Meeting.

4. The participants had a general exchange of views.

5. In accordance with the Concluding Document of the Belgrade Meeting 1977 all the non-participating Mediterranean States were invited to contribute to the work of the Meeting. Egypt and Israel accepted and made their contributions in plenary on 21 February. Syria addressed the plenary on 27 February. The representatives of the United Nations Economic Commission for Europe (ECE),

UNESCO and the United Nations Environment Programme (UNEP) made contributions relating to the work of the Meeting.

6. Two working bodies concerned with co-operation in the economic and in the scientific and cultural fields respectively were established by the plenary and pursued their work under its guidance. The non-participating Mediterranean States which made contributions participated in the discussions of the working bodies. Upon the invitation of the plenary, the representatives of the ECE and UNESCO made additional contributions in the working bodies.

7. The participants stressed the will of their governments to promote the development of good-neighbourly relations and cooperation with the non-participating Mediterranean States and reaffirmed the importance their governments attach to the attainment of the objectives set forth in the Final Act of the CSCE by implementing all of its provisions, as well as their readiness to pursue their efforts accordingly.

8. The participants considered many measures and activities already under way or envisaged, both bilateral and multilateral, relating to mutually beneficial cooperation in the fields of economics, science and culture; in doing so they drew attention to certain current problems in the above-mentioned fields and examined ways of solving them. The participants were of the opinion that the exchange of views which took place in this context was a useful outcome of the Meeting.

9. The Meeting of Experts noted that particularly useful and concrete work in the fields specified in the mandate of the Valletta Meeting is being done by competent international organizations, notably by ECE, UNESCO and UNEP.

10. In accordance with the mandate of the Meeting and taking into account the contributions made at the Meeting by the non-participating Mediterranean States and by the representatives of ECE, UNESCO and UNEP, the participants considered ideas and proposals for further initiatives intended to promote mutually beneficial co-operation in sectors falling within the fields identified for consideration by the Meeting.

11. The Meeting of Experts concluded that for many of those sectors ECE, UNESCO and UNEP provided a framework for

investigating and developing further cooperation among the participating States and the non-participating Mediterranean States, whereas in other sectors unilateral efforts, or bilateral or other forms of multilateral co-operation were more suitable.

12. Accordingly, the participants, having examined the ideas, considerations and proposals which had been submitted, recommend that the Governments of the participating States envisage within their possibilities and interests, through their participation in international organizations and in their bilateral and multilateral relations with the participating States and with the non-participating Mediterranean States, the following:

Economics

13. Continuing their efforts to contribute to the diversified development of the economies of the States concerned, including the non-participating Mediterranean States, taking due account of their national development objectives.

14. Developing the exchange of statistical data, also with the non-participating Mediterranean States, among national statistical institutes, and considering the convening of a meeting of experts within the framework of ECE, with a view to drawing up an inventory of existing data and considering further actions in the fields of data concerning national accounts, labour, agricultural and industrial production, trade, transport, tourism, and environment, education and health.

15. Examining within the framework of UNEP, the possibilities of participating States being provided with information and advice on relevant environmental programmes and activities with a view to achieving better harmonization between Mediterranean and other international programmes; contributing to the efforts to reduce pollution of the Mediterranean; and considering the possibility of developing co-operation initiated within the framework of the Barcelona Convention.

16. Considering the holding of meetings at a technical level, within the framework of the appropriate international organizations, in order to determine the most suitable criteria for making the best possible use of tourist resources and promoting further co-operation

among interested countries in the field of vocational training, in-service training and scholarships.

17. Intensifying the exchange, bilaterally as well as in co-operation with the competent international organizations, of the results of studies on the conservation and rational use of energy and developing their cooperation in the area of solar energy, including with the non-participating Mediterranean States, by supporting the activities of UNEP and taking due account of the outcome of the CSCE "Scientific Forum".

18. Considering the expansion of trans-European and Mediterranean transport networks and promoting with a view to facilitating trade, the further application in these areas of the TIR Convention as well as other instruments and recommendations relating to international transport of goods elaborated within the framework of ECE.

19. Considering co-operation efforts, within the competent international organizations, to adapt agricultural production in the Mediterranean to meet existing needs.

20. Urging better co-operation among the participating States and the non-participating Mediterranean States in the field of fisheries in the Mediterranean, and supporting further studies within competent international organizations on fish processing.

21. Supporting the programme sponsored by UNEP for the development of aquaculture in the Mediterranean as a cooperative project between all interested countries.

22. Promoting co-operation in the field of telecommunications technology among appropriate institutions or firms of interested participating States and non-participating Mediterranean States through the carrying out of joint research, including on new equipment and current technology, the exchange of information, the organization of training courses for specialists, in co-operation with the International Telecommunication Union. Studying the possibility of convening a meeting of experts of interested countries on telecommunications in the Mediterranean.

23. Recommending the host countries and the countries of origin to intensify their contacts with a view to finding solutions to the problems which exist in the field of migrant labour. While fully implementing the existing agreements to which they are parties,

they should also continue, by all appropriate means, their efforts to improve the situation of migrant workers in conformity with the provisions of the Final Act on migrant labour, including the solution of the problems in the economic, social, human and other fields.

Science

24. Practising more widely the holding, within the framework of the competent international organizations mentioned in the Final Act, of conferences, symposia and meetings on the most pressing scientific and technical problems of the Mediterranean that are of general interest.
25. Reinforcing their co-operation in controlling and eradicating certain diseases prevalent in the Mediterranean (e.g. thalassaemia), facilitating studies and conferences, particularly under the aegis of the World Health Organization, with a view to establishing programmes for the prevention, detection and treatment of these diseases and for the training of specialized personnel, on the basis of the expertise which some participating States could share with other countries.
26. Urging further exchanges of views within the competent international organizations, on co-operative studies on gerontology, including environmental geriatric care.
27. Considering the convening under the aegis of the competent international organizations of a scientific conference on the protection of the Mediterranean ecosystem, particularly with a view to studying co-operative projects in the fields of afforestation, forest management, management of water resources, reclamation of arid and semi-arid areas, and drawing up an inventory of the technical centres for research existing in these areas.
28. Developing co-operation in the field of seismology, to increase the exchange of information on seismic phenomena in the Mediterranean and adjacent areas, and considering the convening, under the aegis of UNESCO, of a symposium on seismicity in the Mediterranean and its repercussions in Europe and Africa.
29. Studying with co-operation among the participating States and non-participating Mediterranean States the possibility of the

drafting of a comprehensive history of the Mediterranean utilizing the valuable experience of UNESCO and under its aegis.
30. Encouraging studies relevant to the needs of the Mediterranean, particularly in the fields of science and technology.

Culture

31. Supporting the holding of congresses and conferences by existing international organizations in the field of culture, both in the participating States and in the non-participating Mediterranean States.
32. Increasing their co-operation, both at the bilateral and multilateral level, including within the competent international organizations in the field of scientific research and in the protection and preservation of the cultural and historical heritage of the Mediterranean, notably archaeological and architectural remains, with a view to developing in particular underwater archaeological research and harmonizing the legal and technical modalities for the protection and preservation of this heritage.
33. Considering the preparation of a study on the relationship between the development of tourism in the Mediterranean and the protection, preservation and presentation of the cultural and historical heritage, with the participation of interested participating and non-participating States, and in collaboration with competent international organizations.
34. Expanding their co-operation in the field of the dissemination of scientific and cultural knowledge through radio and television; increasing the exchanges of scientific and cultural radio and television programmes; studying the possibilities, in collaboration with the competent international organizations, of using radio and television for vocational and adult training.
35. Promoting the exchange of films among the film libraries of the participating States and the non-participating Mediterranean States and the holding of Film Weeks.
36. Encouraging the efforts of UNESCO to help Mediterranean countries establish a Mediterranean Cultural Centre.
37. The participants recommend to the Governments of the participating States of the CSCE that they take into account, as

appropriate, at the Madrid Meeting, the results of the Valletta Meeting and that they be mindful in the interim of the outcome achieved by unilateral efforts and within the framework of competent international organizations and in bilateral or multilateral co-operation, in the fields of the mandate for the Valletta Meeting.

38. The participants expressed their deep gratitude to the Government and the people of Malta for the excellent organization of the Meeting and for the warm hospitality extended to them during their stay in Valletta.

26 March 1979

COLOPHON

letter: baskerville 11/13 and 9/11
setter: H. Charlesworth
printer: Princo, Culemborg
binder: Callenbach
cover-design: J. v.d. Bijl